Transforming the World

The Jewish Impact on Modernity

by Leo Dee

URIM PUBLICATIONS
Jerusalem · New York

Transforming the World: The Jewish Impact on Modernity
by Leo Dee

Revised, second edition in softcover

Copyright © 2023, 2016 Leo Dee

Typeset by Ariel Walden

Printed in Israel

ISBN 978-965-524-372-7

Urim Publications, P.O. Box 52287
Jerusalem 9152102 Israel

www.UrimPublications.com

Library of Congress Cataloging-in-Publication Data

Names: Dee, Leo Mark, 1971- author
Title: Transforming the world : the Jewish impact on modernity / Leo Dee.
Description: Jerusalem ; Brooklyn, NY : Urim Publications, [2016] | 2016
Identifiers: LCCN 2015036978 | ISBN 9789655242140 (hardback)
Subjects: LCSH: Judaism—Essence, genius, nature. | Judaism—History of
    doctrines. | Happiness—Religious aspects—Judaism. | BISAC: RELIGION /
    Judaism / Rituals & Practice. | RELIGION / Judaism / Theology.
Classification: LCC BM562 .D44 2016 | DDC 296.3/8—DC23 LC record
    available at http://lccn.loc.gov/2015036978

ORIGINAL DEDICATION (2016)

For my beautiful wife LUCY

and my remarkable children
MAIA, KEREN, TALI, RINA, and YEHUDA

you are my inspiration.

DEDICATION FOR THE REVISED EDITION (2023)

For KEREN, TALI and YEHUDA –
thank you for proving just how remarkable you are.

And for LUCY, MAIA and RINA –
your memory is a blessing to us all.

You all continue to be my inspiration.

CONTENTS

Chapter

ACKNOWLEDGEMENTS

I wish to thank my teachers Rabbi Shlomo Riskin, Rabbi Chaim Brovender, Rabbi Shuki Reich, Rabbi Menachem Schrader, and Rabbi Yitzchak Blau. My intense years of Torah study at Yeshivat HaMivtar were the most thought-provoking of my life.

I am grateful to Rabbi Mordechai Ginsbury of Hendon United Synagogue, and his Executive Board of 2008, who granted me my first opportunity to serve within the British community. I am also indebted to the wonderful community of Radlett United Synagogue that embraced me as their Rabbi for a number of years and welcomed my family into their hearts. In addition, I am thankful to Sam Lyons and Harvey Freeman for their editing input.

I offer my gratitude to my beloved family, to my parents and sister for the wonderful and varied experiences that they exposed me to in my youth and for my parents' helpful comments on the first manuscript. My greatest thanks go to my better half, Lucy, who encourages me to question myself, life, the universe, and everything on an ongoing basis.

Most of all, I would like to thank the Almighty for His kindness in planting me into my parental home, introducing me to my *beschert*, blessing me with five loving and inquiring offspring, granting me a diverse experience of life, and giving me, and all the world, His book – the Torah – which contains all the answers for those who are prepared to search.

כִּי מִצִּיּוֹן תֵּצֵא תוֹרָה וּדְבַר ה' מִירוּשָׁלָם

INTRODUCTION TO THE
SECOND EDITION

Dear Reader,

When I wrote this book and published it in 2016, I could never have imagined what would happen to my family seven years later. Our tragedy struck on April 7, 2023. Lucy, Maia, and Rina were traveling together and Tali, Yehuda, and I were in another car. We were on our way up to the Sea of Galilee for the Passover holiday. Keren had been dropped off in Jerusalem for Shabbat to work at a youth home (for her National Service volunteering). In a few seconds, around 10:52 in the morning, two Palestinian terrorists, funded by Iran, pumped twenty bullets into my wife and two beautiful daughters at close range. Our family would never be the same again.

Although I have an explanation in the original introduction as to what made me write this book (see the original 2016 introduction which follows), I will give a different explanation here as to how this book came about. Both explanations are true. It's a little like our accounts of how Lucy and I first met and fell in love – two stories, two continents, two explanations – but one truth. As I explain later in the book, the Hebrew word for truth (*Emet* אמת) consists of the first, middle, and last letters of the Hebrew alphabet, which illustrates beautifully how truth is seeing the full picture. This explanation is a part of that full picture.

Lucy and I arrived in the Radlett, England, community in 2011 as Senior Rebbitzen and Rabbi (I mention Lucy first as her job was far more important than mine). The community had 2,000 souls and only 1% were traditionally observant. I say "traditionally observant" because they were less particular about the "traditionally observant" *mitzvot* such as Shabbat and eating strictly kosher. However, they were "very observant" of the *mitzvot* of loving one's neighbor, visiting the sick, and giving *tzedakah* (charity).

We were blessed (we thought "appointed by God") to have 150 Bar and Bat Mitzvahs during our three years in the community, literally one per week. We both saw these kids as our calling in the community and decided to invest most of our energies toward preparing them for life as Jewish adults. Lucy and I created and ran a weekly program of courses for fifty Bar and Bat Mitzvahs each year. I insisted on learning one-on-one on two occasions with each Bar Mitzvah boy before his big day. This was a huge investment of my time.

Which topic should I learn with a Bar Mitzvah boy who would most likely not return to synagogue after his Bar Mitzvah, perhaps not until his wedding (if he married a Jewish girl which was not the trend in this community)? I decided there was only one topic which mattered: "Why be Jewish?" And as I had two sessions with each Bar Mitzvah, I split it into two topics:

1) What does Judaism do for me in my life?

2) What do Jews do for the world by keeping the Torah?

Having given these two sessions over seventy-five times in three years, when I came to Israel I decided to publish them.

While writing and analyzing them, I discovered something that I had not fully understood until then. The answer to both questions was the same – SHALOM. Shalom (usually translated inaccurately as "peace") is the bottom line of all Jewish prayers – the *Amidah*, Grace after Meals, the Priestly Blessing, Kaddish, and more. And the answers to the two existential questions of Judaism were: Judaism gives me Shalom (peace of mind or happiness) and Jews create Shalom in the world.

Thus, this book sets out to explain how a diverse set of 613 *mitzvot* (commandments) in the Torah could lead to personal Shalom and world Shalom.

Lucy, Maia and Rina's lives were ended in *Kiddush HaShem*. Lucy extended her *chesed*, giving of herself, in order that five others may continue to live or improve their quality of life. I dedicate the rest of my life to helping spread Shalom (personal, family, community, national, and international), and I hope that this book will inspire generations of Jews to understand their role in the most important project of mankind, given to us by God Himself 3,500 years ago.

May we all be partners for Shalom in each others' lives and in the Universe.

Amen.

Leo Dee
Efrat, June 2023

INTRODUCTION

The setting: The Radlett Centre, a modern theater complex in a small village in the British county of Hertfordshire.

The audience is packed full of four hundred or more Jews of all ages, many with their hands thrust into the air. One is chosen to ask the opening question.

The young man, a science student at a good British university, asks his question:

"Rabbi, isn't the Torah just an ancient text that is out of date and irrelevant in our modern age?"

There is a pause, a tangible hush throughout the auditorium.

And the Rabbi is expected to answer . . .

But, first, back to the beginning.

I didn't have to become a Rabbi. By the age of fifteen I showed signs of being an accomplished scientist. Achieving top grades in my "A" levels, the final high school exams in Britain, I was sent to Cambridge.

"Sent" being the correct term. When you obtain a place at such an institution, you don't have much say in the decision of whether or not to take it up. The decision is made.

After four years of Natural Sciences and Chemical Engineering, I graduated with a top first and a National Prize from the Salters Guild (an ancient British institution), which expected me to become a name within the world of engineering.

But fate, again, took its turn. I found myself being swept into the world of strategy consulting and high finance, buying and selling businesses for millions of pounds and sitting on executive boards, all before I was thirty.

And then, fortuitously, I took a year off to travel the Third World with my wife. Quitting our jobs, we travelled through most of Asia and much of Central and South America – by bus.

The world opened up. Literally. Our perspectives on life had previously been defined by a limited exposure to homo *sapiens*, i.e., to educated man, through our sojourn at blue-chip universities. Now our perspectives were challenged to their core.

Suddenly, not everyone we met had a degree from Oxbridge. Not everyone we met was struggling to pay off a mortgage in a smart London suburb. Not everyone we met was aspiring to be a doctor, lawyer, or accountant.

And yet, we saw glimpses of happiness. Not everywhere, but glimpses: on the faces of children in remote Indian villages, dancing outside their shanty homes; on the faces of remote tribes in Northern Laos, adorned with their golden coin headdresses and straw skirts; and on the faces of villagers in the Peruvian mountains, tending their flocks of alpacas.

The stressful life of London for a "high flier," accumulating as much wealth as possible before dying of an early heart attack, was challenged by these encounters.

And we decided, in our naivety, that there must be more to life.

But where to find it in North West London?

And so, after a few more years of returning to the grindstone, we fled to Israel to study in yeshiva and seminary, two young daughters in arms.

Some forty-eight months later, not only had I learnt more than I had in my previous thirty-two years, but I was also privileged to leave with a rabbinical qualification, two more children, and a fifth on the way.

Back in Britain, I apprenticed for three years with a wonderful mentor, Rabbi Mordechai Ginsbury, in Hendon Synagogue. Now I was ready to take on a Senior Rabbi position of my own, at a growing community named Radlett.

Radlett is an anomaly in the Jewish world, a quaint, and reasonably typical, British village in South Hertfordshire. Twenty years ago most of the residents would never have met a Jew in their lives. And then things began to change.

The direct train line into the City of London, a half-hour journey, led a number of Jewish families to sell their homes in Jewish North London and move a little further out to enjoy the country air, buying much larger homes for the same money.

As with many things in the Jewish world, a good thing doesn't take much time to become a widely known thing. Soon, house prices in Radlett reached central London levels and beyond as Jews flooded into this now-developing town.

Extensions were built to houses. Bungalows were converted into three-story mansions. Four-wheel-drive vehicles were used for shopping sorties to the high street. The Jews had arrived!

One of the first things that the Jews created in Radlett was the synagogue. The old town hall was converted into a shul and the first Orthodox Radlett Rabbi was selected. Three Rabbis later, that Radlett Rabbi was me.

Radlett is a wonderful community, full of *mentschen*. The level of *chesed*, kindness, that is engaged in, within the community and outside it, is incredible. People in Radlett are not conventionally observant (perhaps around 1% are fully Shabbat compliant), but they are religious in many other ways.

This chilly Yom Kippur afternoon in question, I was standing on the stage of the Radlett Centre, where we were holding one of our two overflow services. Between the second and third services of the day, with the aid of some rapid praying, we had two hours for a Question-and-Answer session with the Rabbi.

Many people attended this session. It was standing-room only and silent enough to hear a pin drop. I am not naïve enough to believe that they came in order to hear my pearls of wisdom; in all probability it was less tiring on a fast day to remain in shul, than to return home for a sleep, and hungry people don't tend to chat as much as those who have full stomachs.

In any case, it was the greatest opportunity for Jewish learning throughout the year and, best of all, the topics were chosen by the crowd.

This year in question, I was given the greatest opening that a Rabbi could have.

"Rabbi, isn't the Torah just an ancient text that is out of date and irrelevant in our modern age?"

Suddenly, I realized that all the sermons, all the classes, and all the programming that I and my creative wife Lucy had provided, might have been for nothing.

Here was a young single man, from a substantially involved family within the community, and he was asking such a basic question, that it made any other topic that I might choose to dwell upon, well, irrelevant.

And this question was clearly not just on *his* mind. In the micro-second after he uttered those words, I sensed a level of relieved endorsement from within the packed auditorium. This was clearly a question that others had wanted to ask, but none had had the guts to pose.

So, what is the relevance of a book that is over three millennia old?

And what is the purpose of being a Jew in our modern age?

And why should this generation of Jewish children marry only other Jews, when there are so many people today, of other faiths, who share so many of our values?

To those who secretly harbor these questions, and to those who are brave enough to ask them, and to all my Bar Mitzvah students with whom I pored over these questions, I dedicate this book.

May we merit to have Jewish children and grandchildren and may we never cease asking the most essential questions of life.

PREFACE

Transforming the World, or in Hebrew, "Tikun Olam BeMalchut Shadai."

That's the task set out for Jews and repeated three times daily at the end of our prayers.[1]

But what does it mean?

In this book, I'd like to address the following three questions:

How does the Torah transform my life for the better?

How does the Torah transform the wider world for the better? And,

What is the future for the Jewish people in a modern world?

This book is therefore structured into three sections. Sections One and Two tackle the questions of how the Torah transforms us and the world. Section Three looks to the future.

---

1. In the Aleinu prayer

HOW DOES THE TORAH TRANSFORM MY LIFE FOR THE BETTER?

Chapter 1

WHAT'S IN IT FOR ME?

There is a question that we don't ask frequently enough in life, and that is "Why?"

From an early age, we are channeled into school to learn to read, write, and count.

Later on we learn history, geography, science, algebra, and perhaps another language or two.

But how often do we think "Why?"

Why is it that my parents sent me to school in the first place?

Why was there an unspoken expectation that I would go onto higher education if I could afford it, or tolerate it?

Why did I study the subjects I studied, and not palaeontology, zoology, and advanced internet gaming?

And when I've asked the question, "Why are you studying all these subjects?" to those in the midst of their high school education, the answer is invariably "In order to pass my exams."

And usually the conversation continues as follows:

"And why do you need to pass your exams?"

"In order to go to university."

"And why would you want go to university?"

"So I can get a job."

"And if you got a job – what then?"

"Then I'll make money!"

"And if you have money, so what?"

"Then I can buy the things that I need and that I want!"

"And, if you can buy the things that you want, so what will that do for you?"

After a long pause, the answer is invariably . . .

"Then I will be happy!"

And there we have it.

As humans, we are no different from other animals. Ultimately all we seek is happiness.

Chapter 2

THE GREATEST HAPPINESS

To get a dog or cat to behave in the way that we wish, we feed them treats. If they can associate actions with pleasure, the pleasure of eating their treats, then they will do almost anything for us.

And we're no different.

Jeremy Bentham and his student, John Stuart Mill, developed the "Greatest Happiness Theory" in the late 18th and early 19th century. They stated that man should seek to create the greatest amount of pleasure while minimizing the amount of pain. And with some important exceptions, that is how most of us seek to live our lives.

So, if we educate ourselves in order to work, and work in order to make money, and make money in order to make ourselves happy, what, then, is the need for religion?

What is the need for Jewish culture and practice? Indeed what is the need for any culture?

And here we must ask a fundamental question.

"Does money make us happy?"

Chapter 3

MONEY ISN'T EVERYTHING

It seems that the very basis of our educational culture is to get employed and to make money. But does money actually make us happy?

This is an age-old question and generally we can make two opposing arguments:

i) "Yes! Of course money makes us happy! And, if not, I'd rather be rich and miserable than poor and miserable!"

ii) "No! Money doesn't make us happy. Look at how many rich celebrities commit suicide. Money so often destroys relationships. Money should be a means to an end, but when it becomes an end in itself – it is evil!"

Indeed, the Rabbis have been having this same argument for thousands of years.

On the one hand . . .

> *Moses was rich because God allowed him to keep the [sapphire] chippings from the Ten Commandments* (Babylonian Talmud Nedarim 35a)

And who, after all, could be a greater role model than Moses?

But on the other hand . . .

> *The more property, the more worries* (Ethics of the Fathers 2:8)

So, that's usually where the conversation ends and not much discussion follows. We generally hold one opinion about the potential of money to make us happy, or the other.

But what if we wanted to find the answer? That would take a large scale survey.

In an ideal world I would confront a thousand people at random, in the street, and ask them two questions: "How happy are you?" and "How much do you earn?" I would then plot a chart of happiness against income and see the result. The problem with this approach is that, certainly in the West, the second question would never get a response and the answer to the first question would depend on what day of the week you approached the candidate and what the person had eaten for breakfast.

Fortunately there has been some interesting research on this topic.

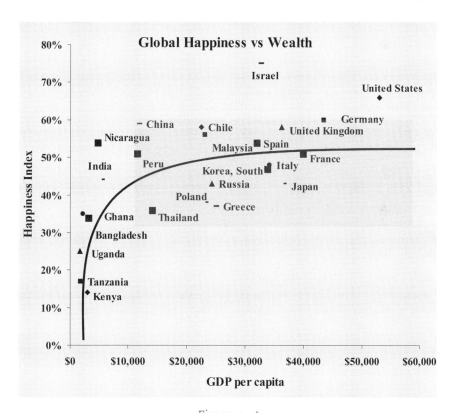

Figure 2.1[1]

---

1.   This research was first presented by Richard Layard, programme director of the Centre of Economic Performance at the London School of Economics, in his book

Psychologists have figured out that getting an accurate answer to the question "does money make you happy?" by asking *individuals* would never work. However, asking the question on a national level does give us a clue to the answer. And that's what we can see in Fig. 2.1 above.

Hundreds of people in tens of countries answered a "Happiness Questionnaire" and so, some of the randomness of the "happiness" question was ironed out. The results were then plotted against the average income per capita for each country. And the results are insightful.

What you see is a steep curve, an increase in happiness, for countries increasing in income from nothing to around $10,000 per head, a reduced curve between $10,000 and $20,000 per head, and then a flattening out of the curve at higher incomes.[2]

In other words:

Money DOES make you happy when you don't have very much of it.

But – money DOES NOT make you any happier when you do!

Consider this:

Chile has an income per head of $22,000 and people in Chile are more than twice as happy as people in Thailand, which has an income of only $12,000 per head.

However, Germans, who are almost twice as wealthy as Chileans, are NO MORE happy!

So once we get to a level of income where we can afford the necessities in life (and these certainly will vary from culture to culture), then extra money doesn't necessarily make us any happier.

If we have food, clothes, a comfortable place to live, perhaps a car and an annual holiday, then any extra money will not necessarily make a difference to our sense of well-being.

Happiness, Penguin 2005. Data has been updated by the author from the Spring 2014 Global Attitudes survey, Pew Research Center and 2014 GDP charts.

2. Note that there is some degree of variance around the trend line. Israel is noticeably happier than expected from comparison to other countries of a similar income. Uplifts in happiness can be achieved through agents other than money, as will be explained in the following chapters.

What an observation for our modern society that puts money-making before almost everything else!

And this was, perhaps, what our Rabbis meant when they said,

> *"One who has 100 (coins) desires 200 and one who has 200 desires 400"*
> *(Kohellet Rabba 1:34)*

In other words, money, when we have a reasonable amount of it (i.e. at least 100 coins), doesn't make us any happier as it only leads us to wanting more. However, when we don't have enough money for our basic existence, we enjoy every extra penny that we obtain.

Chapter 4

HAPPINESS LEVERS

So, for teenagers in the educational system who are likely to find a job that pays above the minimum wage, the question they should be asking themselves is, "If more money won't make me happier, then what will?" And the same question can be asked by those of us who are a few years older.

Or, in other words, we need to ask ourselves: "If I had all the money that I ever needed, what would be the things that would then determine whether or not I was really happy?"

Well, for most people, the following aspects of their lives determine their happiness:

i) Family relationships – "Do I have a home that I am content to come back to each day? How do I get along with my parents, kids, and/or spouse?

ii) Friends – we all need social contact with similar-minded individuals. Whether it's to chat, play games, or go out to a restaurant, human beings mostly hate to be alone all the time. For many of us, friends come predominantly from our places of education – schools and universities – or from our local community.

iii) Time off. I have held a number of highly-pressurized jobs, working around the clock, and when I am exhausted, I find it hard to be happy. Everyone needs time off – an early night, a day or two at the weekend to switch off. Psychiatrists[1] have identified that one of the greatest causes of depression is lack of sleep. And we know it, intrinsically, because whenever we have a late night, we feel groggy in the morning. Regular breaks during the day can also contribute greatly to our happiness.

1. Dr James Gangwisch, "Sleep deprivation and depression", Jan 2010, Sleep Journal

iv) Meaningful occupation. I often ask people, "Would you be happy being paid £1 million a year to screw lids on toothpaste tubes in a noisy factory?" Now, we could all do with that sort of money, but most of us would prefer, if we had a choice, to earn it in a more fulfilling way. And if we were to consider what makes an occupation fulfilling, it should comprise some, or all, of the following:

a. Our occupation should have a LEARNING component. We don't need to be challenged every day but, as human beings, we like to progress and to learn new things.

b. Our occupation should be HELPFUL to others. Something that locks us in a room for days on end without anything to show for it, is not as satisfying as spending our time bringing joy to others. Consider the satisfaction of healing others or feeding them or producing other goods or services that enhance people's lives.

c. Our occupation should be a MATCH with our unique skill set, ambitions and aspirations. One of the greatest satisfactions in our lives is achieving something, and believing that we were one of the very few people in the world who had the skills to accomplish it.

The list goes on, but this is a pretty good start.

So where does Judaism come in to all this?

Well, here's the incredible observation:

Judaism offers us the optimum way to enjoy our lives!

How?

Through commanding us to do things that MAKE US HAPPY!

Let's consider these "Happiness Levers," one by one.

Chapter 5

HAPPY FAMILIES

*"Children are a gift from God . . . Happy is the person who fills his
quiver with them . . ."*
(Psalms 127)

Family is one of the most important ingredients of our happiness.

The amount of time we spend with spouse and children is so immense that if it is enjoyable, it can tremendously enhance our lives. Conversely, if we fear coming home from work, being confronted by an angry spouse and disrespectful children, then a dysfunctional family environment can be one of the greatest sources of our discontent.

What is the ultimate source of family happiness?

Well, every relationship within a nuclear family is important – between siblings and between parent and child. But there is one relationship that is fundamental to creating a strong unit. And that is between husband and wife.

As our Rabbis stated,

*"A man without a wife lives without blessing, life, happiness, help,
goodness, and peace . . . ."* (Babylonian Talmud *Yevamot* 62b)

Two-parent families, where the couple bring up the children in a loving, supportive environment, are consistently demonstrated to be the happiest family structure.[1]

---

1. Cockett and Tripp, *The Exeter Family Study: Family Breakdown and Its Impact on Children*, p. 19, 1994. And Meltzer, H., et al., *Mental Health of Children and Adolescents in Great Britain*, London: The Stationery Office, 2000.

In society, the greatest success factor in keeping parents together in a marriage has been the wedding ceremony, and more specifically the marriage certificate and the associated rights that are given, primarily, to the wife.[2]

Historically the woman was always the weaker partner in a marriage. Once she was pregnant, or with young children, she would struggle to earn a living. Therefore her livelihood was very much in the hands of her husband.

In some societies, historically, and even today, husbands have taken advantage of this biological edge and forced their wives to become subservient, even slaves.

This is not just prejudicial to women and immoral, but it also is destructive towards society as a whole. Women have so much to offer society, through taking an equal role in building it. At least 50% of women are brighter than men[3] and the inequality of women has been a major factor in keeping certain societies from advancement.

Enter the Torah. Three thousand, three hundred years ago, the Torah introduced the *ketubah*, the first marriage contract, something that has transformed global society ever since.

And how?

The *ketubah*, and its modern incarnation – the marriage contract – gives women rights in the event that their husband divorces them or dies. It's financial contract that protects the interests of the wife. The *ketubah* is the origin of "alimony" – and the template for all current protection mechanisms of women and children within marriage.

Not only is the woman's financial protection the correct, moral way to behave in the sad eventuality that a marriage breaks up, but it also leads to greater progress for society, as a whole.

How so?

---

2. A study by the Marriage Foundation, 2013. See Telegraph 22/5/13 "Almost no couples with children who stay unmarried stay together, study claims" by John Bingham. The article reports that 93% of teenagers whose parents are still together come from families whose parents are married.
3. James Flynn *Are We Getting Smarter? Rising IQ in the Twenty-First Century*, Cambridge University Press, 2012. Flynn points out that women are now scoring higher in IQ tests than men, for the first time in recorded history.

A man needs an equal partner, not a rag.

God says to Adam at the beginning of the Torah,

> "Eve [the first wife in history] will be a helper against you."
>
> (Bereishit 2:18)

The Rabbis argue as to what this expression "a helper against you" actually means.

One suggestion given by the Rabbis[4] is that a wife helps her husband by disagreeing with him. And when she knows she is right – even hitting him!

Clearly the Rabbis are not advocating violence within a marriage, but the ability to argue, forcefully, for one's own point of view is critical if one is to sustain a long-term relationship.

Disagreement and forcefulness are only available to a wife in a marriage where she has protection against divorce. Otherwise she is forced to submit to her husband's whims.

And, of course, there is nothing better for a man than to have someone who can actually tell him the truth about himself.

– His friends will tell him what he wants to hear (otherwise they will cease to be his friends).

– His parents will tell him how wonderful he is.

– His siblings who are no longer living with him in the same house can congratulate him on his strengths without ever having to criticize him.

Only our spouse tells us the truth, because they have to live with us for the foreseeable future. And it is honest feedback, in a relationship, that leads to both partners becoming better people. Without a sounding board, an honest opinion, we humans are excellent at convincing ourselves that we are perfect. Marriage is the antidote to self-delusion and in its tensions it creates better citizens, not only in parents, but also in the children that emanate from within it.

---

4.   Babylonian Talmud *Yevamot* 63a

As our Rabbis stated,

> *"A man without a wife lives without . . . the ability to improve himself."*
>
> *(Bereishit Rabba 17:2)*

And this applies equally to a woman without a husband.

And critically, the marriage contract, that simple but effective device to create stability in families and a happy home, is a mitzvah, a commandment from the Torah.

The mitzvah of Jewish matrimony leads to greater happiness.

Chapter 6

HAPPY FRIENDS

"There is a friend that sticks closer than a brother."   *(Proverbs 18:24)*

Friends (mostly) make us happy. Friends are an important part of our happiness.

Does the Torah command us to make friends?

Surely the institution of friendship existed long before the Torah?

Does the creation of friendships need intervention from the Torah?

And here the answer is also "Yes!"

At least for those of us whose friends mostly emanate from school, university or the local community.

How can this be?

Let's consider the institution of community.

For many people, their community centers around a place of worship – a church, a mosque, a temple, or a synagogue.

What's the origin of such a structure? The *Mishkan*, the portable Temple, that is first described in the book of Exodus. The term for synagogue in Hebrew is "Beit Knesset" or, literally, a House of Meeting.

Strangely, for a place of worship, the name doesn't attempt to describe God in any way, but just a place that people can come together.

Interestingly, the innovation of the *Mishkan* over the temples of earlier religions was based on an absence rather than a presence. Previous religions would have had a centerpiece in their place of worship – and that would have been their God, an idol, or at least some representation of it. The great innovation of the first monotheistic place of worship, the *Mishkan*, was the absence of such a symbol.

As God states,

"*Make me a Sanctuary, so that I can live inside of YOU.*" *(Shemot 25:8)*

The *Mishkan* was a place for *us* to get closer to God, not a place in which God would reside.

In the outer courtyard of idolatrous temples there was an altar, where food would be offered to the Deity – pancakes, meat, etc. This was true in the *Mishkan*, too, however there was just one thing missing – the Deity!

The *Mishkan* had an altar in the outer courtyard, and a golden table, incense altar, and candelabra in the middle courtyard. And in the central hub (the Holy of Holies) was the ark containing the stone tablets and the first Torah scroll written by Moses, BUT NO IDOL!

The Holy of Holies (*Kodesh Kodashim*) was the holiest place in the whole world. And it was visited only once a year by the holiest man, the High Priest, on the holiest day, Yom Kippur (see Chapter 12).

Clearly the Temple was a place of holiness. But what is the meaning of holiness?" Answers Rav Abraham Kook[1] (Chief Rabbi of Palestine in the 1920s), holiness is doing things for OTHERS, not just yourself. The Holy of Holies was holy because it was a place that the High Priest atoned for the sins of ALL the people (in the Jewish community and in the world). He was holy because he risked his life to do so (if he had any mishap in the ritual, he risked being consumed by a heavenly fire). And Yom Kippur is a holy day because it is a day that we pray, not just for ourselves, but for all of mankind.

Holiness in Judaism, in general, and in the *Mishkan* in particular, is about other people. So it is no surprise that the modern-day synagogue, along with other monotheistic places of worship, is based upon communal interaction and support. Educational classes, social

---

1. Commentary on the Siddur, *Olat Reiyah.*

events, charities and support groups are all the result of this approach to Godliness.

And so, when the Torah commands us to build places of worship and to pray as a community, it is also commanding the creation of friendships based on mutual understanding and common interests.

There is a common misconception that religious communities tend to cut themselves off from the rest of society and therefore are less socially interactive than more diverse communities.

Interestingly, Robert Putnam, Professor of Public Policy, Harvard University, counters this claim, writing:

> *Religions make Americans into better neighbors and better citizens . . . Ethnic diversity has the opposite effect . . . Diversity seems to trigger not in-group / out-group division, but anomie or social isolation. In colloquial language, people living in ethnically diverse settings appear to "hunker down" – that is, to pull in like a turtle.*[2]

Communities improve the social life of the people within them and, astonishingly, between them and other communities as well.

---

2. Robert Putnam, *Bowling Alone*, p. 308, New York: Simon & Schuster, 2000.

Chapter 7

SCHOOL FRIENDS

"None is poorer than he who lacks knowledge"

(Babylonian Talmud Nedarim 41a)

While for many people their religious community is the source of their deepest friendships, for many others the majority of their close friendships have been derived through school, university, or at the gates of their children's schools.

So does the Torah aid our happiness through enabling these types of friendships?

And here the answer is startling, once again.

If we asked ourselves how long schooling has been available to all children, irrespective of class or background, in the West, we might assume that it has been that way for hundreds of years. In the deepest parts of Africa and Asia we may be aware that some children are sent to work in sweatshops from the age of five, but surely this was not the case in civilized Europe and America for millennia?

And our assumption turns out to be incorrect.

State schooling has only been available to all children in the United Kingdom since the Victorian era, just over 100 years ago, and similarly in the United States and Europe. Before that, even during the late 19th century, many children from poor families would have worked in mines or factories, often in treacherous conditions.

However, in the Jewish world, this was not the case. The Talmud tells us of a discussion that took place, some one-and-half thousand years ago, between Rabbis regarding the importance of primary school education. In the end, they agreed that children from age six and upwards should be required to attend school, EVEN IF THEIR

PARENTS COULD NOT AFFORD IT.[1] And so, they mandated each Jewish village to hold classes for children between 6–13 years of age (with a maximum class size of thirty!), with poorer children's fees being covered by the local community.

And hence, the institution of public (i.e. State) schooling was born – from the Jews.

As for university, the traditional *yeshivot* (places of adult learning of Jewish core texts) formed the template of the modern universities. The oldest secular universities, Oxford and Cambridge, date back to the late Middle Ages. They began as places of learning of core Christian texts (i.e. the Bible) in Hebrew and Greek. Originally, university professors were required to study Biblical Hebrew as a basic entry criterion.

I recall a fascinating conversation I had as a student at Cambridge University, over Shabbat dinner with an Israeli postgraduate student named Boaz. He told me that a few years back (in the late 1980s) he was sitting in the Hebrew University library in Jerusalem when he was approached by a young Frenchman, a student of theology, who asked him to translate an ancient manuscript written in Hebrew.

Boaz duly complied and translated the text that consisted of diverse quotations and arguments from the Babylonian Talmud. When he eventually asked who had written this manuscript, he was amazed to hear that it was none other than Sir Isaac Newton, the founder of physics and modern science. Apparently, Boaz explained to me, a fact that I have since confirmed through my own research, the Hebrew manuscripts of Sir Isaac Newton were purchased in 1936 by a scholar of Jewish Oriental Studies, Abraham Shalom Yahuda. Yahuda then donated these manuscripts to the Hebrew University in Jerusalem on his death in 1951.

Boaz recounted how he made a list of all the Talmudic references within Newton's manuscripts and took them to a friend, studying at the Mir Yeshiva in Jerusalem. Without revealing the identity of the Torah student, Boaz asked him what level of Jewish knowledge could be ascribed to someone who had studied such a wide range of rabbinical sources. The answer astonished him. His friend replied,

---

1.   Babylonian Talmud, *Baba Batra* 21a.

"The person who studied these sources has a level of knowledge that is way beyond that of a modern-day Rabbi!"

Newton himself allegedly attributed his calculation of the Gravitational Constant to his analysis of the dimensions of the *Mishkan* given in the Talmud. And his biographer, John Maynard Keynes, opens his section on the "Theology of Isaac Newton" with the following statement,

"Newton was . . . a Judaic monotheist of the school of Maimonides."

None other than Albert Einstein congratulated Yahuda on his donation of the manuscripts to the Hebrew University, writing,

My Dear Yahuda,

Newton's writings on biblical matters seem to me particularly interesting because they afford deep insight into the unique mind and thought process of this great man. The divine origin of the Bible is, for Newton, absolutely certain . . . This confidence led him to the firm conviction that the seemingly opaque parts of the Bible must contain important revelations, the clarification of which can only be achieved by deciphering the Bible's symbolic language. Newton pursued this decipherment, i.e., this interpretation, by means of incisive, systematic thinking and meticulous utilization of every possible source . . .

A. Einstein[2]

Sir Isaac Newton, the 17th century Professor of Physics at Cambridge University, was a top Hebrew scholar with a Jewish outlook on life. He arrived at his theological and scientific understanding aided substantially by his analysis of Torah texts. Indeed, on his death, the largest section of his personal library consisted of Jewish Rabbinical writings.[3]

In any case, it is clear that the modern university, with its initial focus on theology, and even its later move into the sphere of science, came about through the agency of the Torah.

---

2. Albert Einstein Archives, The Hebrew University of Jerusalem, September 1940.
3. John Harrison, *The Library of Isaac Newton*, Cambridge University Press, 1978.

The mitzvah of studying and of building places of education is firmly based in the Torah. And so too, for many of us, it is also the source of our closest friendships and happiness.

Chapter 8

HAPPY DAYS

"Six days you shall do all your work, but the seventh shall be a Sabbath for the Lord your God, you shall do no work – neither you, your children, your servants, your animals nor the foreigner in your town."
(Shemot 20)

What about another source of our happiness – time off?

Surely taking time off from work is a natural part of life. Surely one cannot claim that having time off is just another mitzvah, another Torah commandment?

And here the answer is, again, "Yes you can!"

If we took ourselves back over three and half thousand years in history, we would find societies based firmly on slavery. After all, there have always been the stronger and the weaker in society, and in cultures where there are no other controls, the weak are usually forced to work while the powerful sit back and relax.

And so, if we were to ask the origin of a "day off" in history, we'd have to revert back to the Torah.

The fourth of the Ten Commandments states that we must keep the Sabbath along with our animals, Jewish and non-Jewish servants. In other words, the Torah mandates a DAY OFF. Not just for the rich and powerful, not even just for Jews, but for *everyone* within society. For the first time in history, people were given the right to a day off.

And Shabbat, the Jewish Sabbath, is not just "a" day off. It is *the* day off, for the whole community. And that is the secret of the joy that one can derive from a Sabbath day. A shift worker may have Tuesday as his day off, but that is not a "Sabbath" day. What makes the Sabbath special is that the whole community has the same day.

We can invite friends and family for celebratory meals. We can sit at home and chat or stroll in the parks, and the atmosphere is relaxed. The concept of a global day off is irrational from a simple humanistic standpoint – surely it would be more economically efficient to stagger days off through the week and maintain production in businesses and services to customers? It takes Divine wisdom to decree that our sanity is best preserved only when we take a day off along with the rest of Creation.

And if we were to think that the weekend was enshrined in pre-history, we would be wrong. Consider the word for "Saturday" in other languages: for example, Italian and Spanish. In Italian, "Saturday" is "Sabato" and in Spanish it is "Sabado." Both these names clearly derive from the Hebrew word for the Sabbath, "Shabbat." Now, one might ask, why would two Christian Nations, both firmly founded on Roman Catholic principles, call "Saturday" the "Sabbath?" Surely for Christians the Sabbath is on Sunday?

And, here, one can see the origin of the weekend. The first ever day off was Saturday and so it found its way into Roman, and early Christian, language and culture. At some point the Christian Sabbath was moved to Sunday, but apparently too late in Italian and Spanish society to shift the day's name.

In Arabic too, Saturday is "yawm al-sabt" – the Sabbath day. When Friday was eventually appointed the Muslim Sabbath, it was also too late for this to be incorporated into the vernacular.

So aside from 15 million Jews, there are 2.2 billion Christians and 1.6 billion Muslims – well over 50% of the world's population – who owe their weekend directly to the Torah and the mitzvah of Shabbat. And with them, the rest of the world that enjoys this same weekend, owes this indirectly to the Torah.

Time off is a mitzvah, a Divine commandment, and one of the most important contributions to global and personal happiness.

Chapter 9

MEANINGFUL WORK

"Great is work for it honors the workman" (Babylonian Talmud
Nedarim 49b)

"When you eat the toil of your labor – happy you shall be!" (Psalms
128:2)

Another major component of our happiness is being engaged in meaningful work. And the three greatest elements that contribute to our work being meaningful are:

A) That it has a learning component

B) That it feels intrinsically as though it is a match with our particular strengths and desires

C) That we feel that it helps others

A. ONGOING LEARNING

As far as ongoing learning is concerned, we have already discussed that learning is a mitzvah.

B. MATCHING OUR STRENGTHS

As far as matching our work with our personality, this is also a mitzvah. The ultimate prayer that we make each day is for "*Shalom.*" "*Shalom*" is usually translated as "peace." But the word "*Shalom*" is actually connected to the Hebrew word for "completeness." We pray for global peace and we pray for personal peace. Personal peace comes about when we are satisfied with our lives.

Personal peace, *Shalom*, is not about sitting quietly and relaxing. If our lives were a jigsaw puzzle, then Shalom would not be about turning each piece into a boring rectangle that could stack neatly on top of another. It would be about creating a map from all the complex pieces that slot into each other and make a bigger, and more beautiful, whole.

We are at peace with ourselves when we feel that we are achieving something that is uniquely ours.

The great Rabbi Grossman of Migdal Ha'Emek (a town in Northern Israel), transformed a squalid Israeli city into a center of excellence for youth and learning. He was once asked a fascinating question.

> *Standing in his black hat and gown on top of a mountain in the Lower Gallilee, surrounded by hundreds of the youth whose lives he elevated and transformed, he was asked, "Why did you leave the security of Meah Shearim (a religious area in Jerusalem), to come to this Northern town?" And he answered, simply, "I looked at myself, one day, and asked myself the question, "Do they need another one like me, here?" And I honestly had to answer, "No!" So I asked myself, "Where, then, do they need me?"*

"Where do they need me?" a question that our subconscious mind is asking us constantly.

And very often the answer is "not here!" That answer can lead us on to new journeys. Sometimes we have no other choice than to stay put, but our souls will never be at peace until they know that they are being utilized to their full extent.

Personal peace is obtained when we find the task that is uniquely ours, or at least when we embark on the journey to find it. And embarking on that journey is also a mitzvah.

> *"God said to Avram . . . Go to a land that I will show you" (Shemot 12:1). Rashi asks, "Why did God not tell Avram the destination?" and he answers, "In order to make the quest more rewarding."*

C. BEING HELPFUL TO OTHERS

> *Rabbi Beroka asked Elijah the Prophet: "Is there any person in the marketplace who is destined for the world to come [i.e. Paradise]?" He replied, "No." . . . Whilst they were conversing, two people passed*

by. Elijah said, "These two are destined for the world to come!" Rabbi Beroka approached them and asked them what they did. They replied, "We are jesters, and we cheer people up who are depressed. And when we see two people who are quarreling, we work hard to make peace between them." (Babylonian Talmud, Taanit 22a).

Is it a Torah commandment to perform work that is helpful to others?

Would it not be obvious to do this without the Torah's intervention?

And here there is yet another revelation – the source for looking after others in society is a Torah mitzvah.

How do we know this?

Consider the vehicle that has been established, in most cultures, for looking after others – the charitable organization. Simply put, someone collects money in a pot from those with spare change and spends it on those who don't have enough funds.

Collecting and spending.

Simple.

Surely all cultures have been doing this for millennia?

Well, no!

The Greek word "philanthropy" which describes the giving of money for the benefit of others, was used predominantly to describe the sponsoring of sports events and entertainments. Neither the ancient Greeks, nor the ancient Romans, were particularly concerned about the poor, sick, or elderly. Only when early Christian culture took over the Roman Empire did the modern concept of charity begin.

And from where did the Christian concept of charity derive?

From the Old Testament, from the Torah.

Specifically from the commandment to give a tenth of our income, crops and animals, to the poor and the priestly caste.

For thousands of years Jews have separated off a part of their wealth for the benefit of others. The Rambam, Moses Maimonides, the great Rabbi and Spanish philosopher of the 12th century, famously describes one of the highest forms of charity as being:

. . .where the donor does not know who will be the beneficiary and where the beneficiary does not know the identity of the donor.[1]

Hence, through the Torah commandment for looking after the poor and the sick, the concept of charity was born.

The commandments for helping others extend beyond charity in a purely financial sense, to the giving of our time and other resources. There are separate commandments to invite people into our homes, to visit the sick, and to bury the dead.

Overall, helping others is an essential Torah commandment. And ultimately, it leads us towards some of our greatest personal satisfaction in life.

---

1.   See Rambam, *Mishneh Torah*, Laws of Charity 10:7–14

Chapter 10

SPIRITUAL AND MATERIAL JOY

One of the most interesting discussions that I have had with groups of teenagers and their parents is about the source of their greatest happiness.

At numerous seminars on the topic, I have handed out blue Post-it notes to the teens and yellow ones to the parents. And, very simply, I have asked every one of them to write out three things that make them most happy in life, on three separate Post-it notes.

Once I collect the Post-it notes, I then draw on a whiteboard two columns, one entitled "BODY" and the other, "SOUL." And, with the help of the assembled teens and parents, I stick each Post-it note into the appropriate column.

The young teens have typically written that their greatest happiness derives from "computer games," "visits to my favorite restaurant," "football," and "money." The parents have typically identified "time with family," "time with friends," and "seeing smiles on my children's faces" as the sources of their greatest pleasure.

What becomes apparent, very rapidly, is that the majority of pleasures, as identified by the teens', are found on the BODY side of the whiteboard; while the majority of pleasures, as identified by the parents, are located in the SOUL section.

This should not be a surprise. If we took the issue of happiness to an extreme and looked at the widest possible age gap, it is self-evident. A baby starts out with only bodily pleasures and seeks to hold onto everything and put every object into its mouth. A home bound nonagenarian derives most of her pleasure from contact with visitors and living vicariously through her grandchildren and great-grandchildren.

At what point does the switch occur – that we start to appreciate spiritual experiences above bodily pleasures? It seems to be a long process that begins around Bar / Bat Mitzvah, when the child begins to take on more responsibility. But even as adults we may continue to seek pleasure from fast cars, kitchen extensions, and five-star holidays.

When I ask the question "Which pleasure is longer lasting? BODY or SOUL?" I generally get unanimous agreement that soulful pleasures are more sustainable. The memory of our children's first footsteps will probably make a longer lasting impression on us than the taste of foie gras in an expensive restaurant.

Interestingly, many of the Torah commandments can be seen as ways to transform physical pleasures into spiritual experiences – thereby elevating and heightening the level of joy that one can sustain.

For example, Friday night dinner, generally consisting of wine, challah loaves, and a hot meat meal, is elevated from an eating binge to a thanksgiving ceremony for our Creator, through the recital of "*Kiddush*" and "*HaMotzi*," blessings over the wine and bread.

Physical relations between and a man and a woman are elevated from a purely lustful experience to the means of fulfilling God's will in society, through the institution of marriage.

The most materialistic commodity that we possess, money, is transformed from something purely physical to something spiritual through the giving of charity to meaningful causes.

In summary, Torah commandments such as Shabbat, marriage and charity have the power to transform short term physical pleasures into enduring spiritual experiences.

Chapter 11

JEWISH LIFE –
THE SOURCE OF HAPPINESS

Whether by introducing better ways to live our lives or through enhancing those things that we already do, the commandments enable us to derive greater satisfaction from our lives.

One of the great aspects of Jewish life is the amount of joy that can be derived from engaging with Torah ideas and actions. Perhaps this alone has led to the unique longevity of our culture against all odds throughout generations of persecution and assimilation.

In summary, if our first question was "How does the Torah transform my life for the better?" the answer is that Jewish life, with its focus on family, community, education, meaning, and rest is enriching, fulfilling, and gives us the potential to achieve our greatest happiness.

In fact, so many of the things that we may have thought were universal sources of joy turn out to be derived, in one way or another, from the Torah.

i) Marriage, and the nuclear family structure that it creates, has its origins in the Torah

ii) Community, centering around a place of worship, has its origins in the Torah

iii) Education, schools and modern universities, all have their origins in the Torah

iv) Weekends, the time we have to enjoy with family and friends, has its origins in the Torah

v) Charity, giving of our time and resources to others, has its origins in the Torah

vi) The search for meaning, and the ability to transform mundane actions into spiritually uplifting moments, has its origins in the Torah.

In short, the Torah has informed and transformed modern life, for
Jews and for the rest of the world.

So, what is the Jewish impact on modernity?

Jews, through their continued study and observing of the Torah and
its commandments, have introduced mankind to many of its greatest sources of satisfaction and meaning in the current era.

HOW DOES THE TORAH TRANSFORM THE WORLD FOR THE BETTER?

Chapter 12

HAPPINESS IS NOT ENOUGH

Says King Solomon in his book Kohelet:

"Happiness – what does it accomplish?" (Kohelet 2:2)

Happiness is, simply, not enough.

So why is happiness not enough?

In the words of King Solomon:

"The superiority of man over animals is nothing!" (Kohelet 3:19)

His coded answer is that, despite mankind being able to speak and reason, fundamentally we are just animals with animal desires. And, therefore, if our sole pursuit is for happiness we are likely to go astray. Consider the alcoholic and the drug addict who pursue happiness through the use of chemicals in much the same way as an animal pursues its food. Says King Solomon, there must be more to just seeking immediate gratification.

With this in mind, there have been various attempts throughout history to try to classify to what extent the pursuit of happiness should control our lives.

Consider the philosophy of Utilitarianism, one of the earliest attempts to express human morality in the terms of happiness. To Utilitarians, morality is:

"the greatest good for the greatest number" [1]

---

1. Francis Hutcheson, "Inquiry Concerning Moral Good and Evil," 1725.

If this sounds reasonable, then consider the result of this approach to morality.

Jeremy Bentham, who promoted the morality of Hutcheson, suggested that beggars on the streets of London should be rounded up and sent to a workhouse,

"since even though it may reduce the happiness of the few beggars, it would increase the happiness of passers-by who would not feel guilty, and it would reduce the cost to society of giving charity, as the beggars would work to support themselves."[2]

Michael Sandel, Professor of Government at Harvard University, explains that this philosophy of seeking the "greatest good for the greatest number of people" has been used by countless tyrannical regimes to justify genocide. According to this approach, if most people would benefit by the persecution, or enslaving, of a small (or large) minority, then it is morally justified.

That is why pure Utilitarianism, as proposed by Bentham and Hutcheson, was soon replaced by the philosophy of John Stuart Mill.

Mill proposed an adjusted form of utilitarianism that took into account the rights of the minority,

"The only freedom, which deserves the name, is that of pursuing our own good in our own way, so long as we do not attempt to deprive others of theirs, or impede their efforts to obtain it." (John Stuart Mill, *On Liberty*, 1859)

In other words, the greatest good for the greatest number of people *without harming others.*

But this approach to morality, too, has its limitations.

If morality is just about increasing happiness, while not disregarding other people's rights to their own happiness, we open the door to some strange anomalies. Consider the following story reported by Michael Sandel,

> In 2001, a strange encounter took place in the German village of Rotenburg. Armin Meiwes, a 42 year old software technician, advertised on the internet for someone who would be willingly killed and eaten.

2. Extract from *Justice: What's the Right Thing to Do?*, Michael Sandel, Farrar and Giroux, 2009.

> A 43 year old Bernt-Jurgen Brandes replied, came to Meiwes farmhouse and gave his written consent to be killed and eaten – which he duly was.
>
> (Miewes, who is now languishing in a German jail, has reportedly become a vegetarian as he believes that factory farming is inhumane!)[3]

Most people would agree that cannibalism, even between consenting adults, is abhorrent and immoral. But what this story shows us is that people can engage in activities that are "happy," even consensual, but which are wrong.

The search for the greatest happiness, even with a concern for individual rights, can sometimes lead to immorality.

What, then, is the morality that leads us to the "good life?"

Answers King Solomon,

"Remember the Creator in the days of your youth" (Kohelet 12:1)

In other words, the search for the "greatest happiness" is justified, but one's time horizon must be extended from the immediate present to well into the future.

If we are just searching for immediate happiness, then even accounting for others' rights, we can end up with immoral outcomes – like consenting cannibalism.

But if we are to take a long-term view – and here King Solomon is not just suggesting one lifetime, but many lifetimes (after all, our Creator is infinite) – then there is a morality based on the "greatest happiness for the greatest number over the greatest period of time" – and that is JUDAISM.

In this model of morality, one doesn't permit consenting adults to pervert morality today, because the impact of their perversion will likely influence others, negatively, in the years to come.

Of course, this form of morality, let us call it "the ultimate happiness," is difficult for us as individuals to define, alone, in our day-to-day lives. How do we quantify what is a "perversion" and how

---

3.   Michael Sandel, *Justice*, 2009.

do we know what will be best for the majority over a protracted period of time?

The answer is: mankind has only one source for this eternal morality and that is the Torah.

The Torah is the best selling book over the past few millennia.

The Torah has been used as the basis for morality for the majority of the world's population for more than one thousand years.

The Torah is the only book of morals that has been constantly studied, by the world's brightest and most educated individuals, for over three thousand years.

The Torah, in its fullest sense, including the rabbinical books of the Mishnah and Talmud, has been kept up-to-date by constant discussion and debate of the greatest minds in history.

And the Torah has a model (THE model) for the greatest human happiness over the greatest period of time.

And that is the subject of our next few chapters.

Chapter 13

PEACE IS EVERYTHING

"Maybe a person will think that since they have food and drink, they have everything . . .but a person who doesn't have peace has nothing at all"　(Sifra BeChukotai 1)

When someone is asked "What is the worst thing that is going on in the world today?" the most popular answer given, in my experience, by nine people out of ten, is "war."

You only have to open a newspaper today to read about fighting in the Middle East, in Africa, and civil unrest in the West. People are being killed in conflicts in countries all around the world that most of us have never heard of and for causes that we hardly understand.

And so, when asked what is the most important thing that one could dedicate one's life to achieving, most people would say "world peace."

Seeing that the quest for peace is so instinctive, one would imagine then, that the majority of good people in the world would choose to be working for world peace, or at least a large minority of them.

But how many of us, really, dedicate our lives to creating world peace?

I mean, we might support the odd charity that helps poor people and war victims in distant parts of the world, but do we really wake up in the morning and think "what can I do for world peace today?"

And if we put our minds to it, how many people can we name who are currently dedicating their lives to creating world peace?

Well, who would we name?

Maybe the leaders of the world's major nations?

The President of the USA or the Prime Minister of Britain?

But do they really work to create world peace? If the economy of America or Britain was at stake, would they make the peaceful decision or the decision that would be best for their own country? Probably the latter and, certainly, we shouldn't ever blame them for working in the short-term best interests of their own citizens, after all they would like to be re-elected within five years.

So who does wake up and jump out of bed each morning to help to create world peace?

The leader of the United Nations or its ambassadors or employees?

In an ideal world, yes. But in reality the United Nations is preoccupied by the political squabbles of its member states and has not contributed dramatically to world peace in its seventy-plus years of existence.

Perhaps we would nominate charity workers or peace troops for this title of "peace makers?" While they certainly play an important role in the arena of peace, they are generally tackling the symptoms, rather than the causes, of war and discontent.

Whose job, then, is it to create world peace on an ongoing basis throughout their lives?

And the startling answer is "the Jewish people."

Now, that's a controversial statement and I wouldn't expect it to go unchallenged.

It is also a conjecture that cannot be proven by the usual form of logic used in our day-to-day lives, namely "deduction." In fact, for major insights into our lives, our Rabbis used the powerful form of logic known as "induction."

Chapter 14

PROVING THE UNPROVABLE

Deductive logic is the ability to work something out, based on other facts that one knows. If I told you that "red hot coals were dangerous" and you came across a sign upon a door in my house that had a vivid picture of red hot coals, then you would likely deduce that entry to that room would be dangerous. That's the power of deduction and most of our studies at school and university are based on deduction.

Our education provides us with a lot of information, formulae and examples – some of these will be directly useful to us in the future but, mostly, we will need to use the techniques and information that we have learned in similar, but not identical, situations using our powers of deduction.

Our Rabbis had a different problem in the period after the destruction of the Temple. For the first time, Jews had been dispersed across the whole world by the Roman Empire. And while the key Jewish laws had been written down in shorthand in the Mishnah, the main discussions and reasons for them had not been noted in that text. What followed in the next 400 years was a long discussion as to the meaning, source, and purpose of these Rabbinic (and Torah) laws – filling in the gaps that had been caused by the destruction and dispersion of so many critical places of Jewish learning.

And the way that the Rabbis derived the meanings, sources, and purpose of the laws was by inductive logic. They took laws from the Mishnah and contemporary texts, known as Braitas, and argued that if the law was such-and-such in one situation and diametrically different in a slightly different situation, then the ultimate reason for this was based on the subtle difference between the two situations. They *induced* reasons for the laws.

For example, if I was told that swimming in seas is dangerous, but swimming in the (land-locked, extra-buoyant) Dead Sea is safe, I could induce that the reason for the generic danger is a strong current (that doesn't exist in a land-locked sea) or, perhaps, a lack of buoyancy.

If we are to "prove" that the Jewish people have been tasked with creating Shalom, peace, in the world, then we, too, will have to engage in inductive logic. We will have to gather together as many facts about the assertion as we can, and induce that there is no more reasonable explanation than the one that we presupposed.

There are two major questions that need to be assessed to "prove" this assertion. Firstly, is peace making really the key role of Jews in the world?

And secondly, if so, how do Jews actually make peace in the world?

Is peace making really the key role of Jews in the world?

To answer this, let's start by considering some facts.

Fact #1.

Jewish liturgy is loaded with prayers for peace – Shalom. More than that, prayers for peace are usually the *final* request in our prayers.

i) The final prayer in the Amidah, the central nineteen blessing prayer that is recited three times daily, is for God to make peace, Shalom.

ii) The final line of the Kaddish prayer, recited regularly by mourners and by the service leader throughout the prayer service, is "*Oseh Shalom Bimromav*" – God make peace.

iii) The final line of our Benching, our Grace after Meals, is "*Hashem Yivarech et Amo BaShalom*" – God bless his nation with peace.

iv) The final verse of the three-part Priestly Blessing is "*Yisa Hashem Panav Eilecha veYasem Lecha Shalom*" – God make peace.

Fact #2.

If we were asked to name three peaceful nations around the world, nations that do not wage war on their neighbors just to seize their land and assets but generally look for peaceful means of co-existing, it is fascinating to note which nations we might name.

Generally the nations of Europe, North and South America, and the Commonwealth are named. These nations have one thing in common, as far as their religious cultures are concerned – and that is: they were founded upon Christian values. These Christian values, of peace, love, and justice are, in turn, based upon good "Old Testament" values – or, in other words, the Torah.

There is hardly a peaceful nation in the world whose culture has not been derived ultimately from the Torah values written down by Moses some three and a half millennia ago.

Fact #3.

Shalom, the Hebrew word for "peace" comes from the root meaning "complete."

As Jews, our view of peace is not a homogeneous group of nations all singing from the same hymnbook, but rather a world where nations retain their individuality, but within a framework where every component can be appreciated for its own contribution.

We end our morning prayers with a quote from the Babylonian Talmud,

> *"Torah scholars increase peace in the world as it is written in Isaiah, "All of Your children are students of God; great is the peace of Your children."*

Says Rav Kook[1], first we must recognize that "all your children" are students of God – in other words, all of mankind is beloved to God. Then we must play our part in the building of peace, with that understanding.

The statement that "Torah scholars increase peace in the world" is particularly bizarre to anyone who has set foot into a Jewish place of learning – a Yeshiva – because a Yeshiva is full of people arguing over texts, frequently with raised voices and passion. However, the Talmud comes to teach us that it is precisely this ability to disagree and to hear another perspective that is the source of peace – the understanding that others have valid opinions that may differ diametrically from our own.

With these facts in mind, let's investigate how, precisely, Judaism has successfully contributed to greater peace in the world.

---

1. Chief Rabbi Palestine in the 1920's. In his book *Ein Ayah*.

Chapter 15

JEWS –
A PERPETUAL MINORITY

How many Jews are there in the world? Often the answer given to this question, by Jews or non-Jews, is a number ranging from 100 million to two billion. But this is not the case. The number of Jews in the world today is approximately 15 million. In a world of seven billion souls, Jews represent a little over 0.2% of the world's population. That means that 99.8% of the world's population is not Jewish.

Fine.

Now let's ask the question, how many commandments are there in the Torah for Jews? And how many for non-Jews?

Well, for Jews the famous number that is often quoted is 613 commandments. This is derived from a Midrash that teaches that the *gematria* (numerical value of the individual letters) in the word "Torah" is 611. Along with the two first commandments that God gave to the Jewish people "verbally" at Mount Sinai, that makes 613 Torah laws for Jews. In practice, there are far more rabbinical laws than Biblical laws – for example the thousands of rabbinical laws pertaining to what is considered forbidden work on Shabbat – and so Jews have thousands upon thousands of laws to learn and to keep.

OK, but what about non-Jews?

How many laws do non-Jews have to keep according to the Torah?

And here the answer is a startling low: SEVEN – the seven Noahide laws.

How do we know this?

Well, the first Jew in the world was Abraham, who "converted" as an adult on his discovery of the One God. Prior to Abraham there were twenty generations of mankind, the most famous people of that period being Adam and Noah. Clearly Adam and Noah were non-Jews, because Judaism didn't exist in any form during their lifetimes. However, there were seven laws given to Adam and Noah in the Torah (according the reckoning of our Rabbis). If so, these seven laws could not have been given to Jews, but to all of mankind (i.e., Jews and non-Jews alike).

So, why would God have given Jews, who represent only 0.2% of the world's population, 613+ laws to keep and to learn, while giving the vast majority of the world's population only seven laws?!!

A cynical answer might be that Jews are the "chosen people" or somehow superior. But this is not the case and it is clear that a righteous non-Jew (i.e., one who keeps his or her seven laws) is on the same level as a righteous Jew (who must keep his or her 613+ laws).

So why the preponderance of laws for Jews?

And why just seven rules for non-Jews?

Let me suggest, in an inductive sort of way, a simple answer.

God wanted all of mankind simply to keep these seven essential laws, Jew and non-Jew alike, and he commissioned the Jewish people to implement them. However, someone who is in charge of the spreading of ideas to others needs a few more rules, of their own, in order to achieve this.

Consider a management consultant who comes into a company to change the way that it operates. His job is to spread good business practice into his client's business. But he, the consultant, must have his own strong code of conduct and methods, in order to make an impact on the business that has employed him. Although he is the minority, he must adhere to strict rules (of consultancy) in order to impact the whole. And ultimately it is the whole that matters most to him – the success of his client.

Similarly, a head teacher who is brought in to turn around a failing school must have her own strict guidelines to adhere to, so that she is not dragged into the lax culture that prevails.

So, too, the role of the Jewish people is to inspire the world to keep the seven basic laws – and therefore the Jewish people have been given many more rules to help them to achieve their goal.

But why, in any case, would God create an imperfect world that needs improvement by man?

A traditional view of the Creation story explains that God created everything up until man. When man was created, God rested. And then what? He left the rest of Creation up to us. When the Torah tells us that man was created in the image of God, that is precisely what it means. Just as God created (perfection), so too we are capable of creating perfection. It just takes us an awful lot longer.

And this is something that forms a pattern in our world. Rabbi Akiva Tatz[1] teaches that according to Jewish mysticism, many "natural" systems work through a flash of Divine inspiration followed by immense human effort.

Consider, for example, love. When a man and woman fall in love, they are swept off their feet and given a glimpse of perfection, such that all they can think about is their faultless partner and perfect life ahead. That's for free – it doesn't take much effort at all to achieve. Once they marry (or move in together) however, that feeling is gradually taken away. And then the true challenge arises – how can they rebuild what they had at the beginning? And the answer is – only through their own hard work.

The same thing occurs when we are learning. Occasionally we experience a flash of inspiration and the feeling that we've really understood something. But then the feeling goes away and we realize that we never fully understood the subject at all. All we know is that if we put some further effort in, we might get back to that perfect feeling of understanding that we had right back at the beginning.

Well, what's true for our experiences is true for Creation, too. We were given a glimpse of Paradise in the Garden of Eden. Why? So that we could spend the rest of human history working out how to return to that perfection that we were shown right back at the beginning.

And that perfection was peace. In fact, the moment that Adam and Eve left the Garden of Eden, we are presented with the murder of

---

1. *Living Inspired*, Akiva Tatz, Feldheim 1993.

Abel by Cain. The first world war – 25% of the world's population annihilated, in just one battle.

In other words, the reason that God created mankind was in order for us to finish His work and to return the world to a state of perfect Peace.

Chapter 16

WHY CAN'T THE WORLD TRANSFORM ITSELF?

So now the question is "Why would God choose a small group of people, the Jews, to teach peace to the world? Why didn't he simply reveal Himself to all of mankind and get them all to keep His laws?"

And the answer can be found at the beginning of the Torah in the story of Noah. The Torah tells us:

> Noah was a righteous and pure man (but) he was with his
> generation.
> (Bereishit 6:9)

Noah failed in his task to help the world. He built an ark which took tens of years, but in the process he didn't manage to convince a single soul that they should mend their ways, and the whole world was destroyed.

Noah was the worst leader that the world has ever known. Under his guard, the whole world was destroyed!

What was Noah's problem? Why couldn't he impact his fellow man? And the answer is right there in his introductory verse: "Noah was WITH his generation".

When you're one of the group, you can't make such an impact, people don't take you seriously. "Oh it's just that Noah guy again! Come on Noah, join us for another game of Poker!" The prophet Jonah, in contrast, comes out of nowhere and transforms the ancient city of Nineveh in an instant – because he's an outsider.

And Abraham, the first Jew, is chosen because he is an "Ivri" – literally "across the way."

> *Everyone walked on one side, and Abraham on the other. He was present, yet apart.* (Midrash Bereishit Rabba 42:8)

And that's the formula for making an impact. To be a part and yet to be separate – all at the same time.

So God's plan was to perfect the world, to bring it to Peace, to Shalom.

And who did He choose for this task? The Jews.

And what was their specific objective? To implement the seven Noahide laws across humanity. Not through force, but through example.

Chapter 17

THE SEVEN LAWS OF HUMANITY

So what are these seven laws, the Noahide laws, that will ultimately bring all of humanity to a state of Peace?

They are as follows:

i) Not to murder
ii) Not to steal
iii) Not to abuse women[1]
iv) To establish a just system of law in every jurisdiction
v) Not to worship idols
vi) Not to curse God's name
vii) Not to tear the limb of a living animal

And to simplify our discussion, let me group them into three logical groups:

A. Crime Prevention	B. Avoiding Cruelty	C. Religion
1. Don't murder	5. Don't tear the limb off a living animal[2]	6. Don't worship idols
2. Don't steal		7. Don't curse God's name
3. Don't abuse women		
4. Set up a legal system		

---

1. This prohibition includes sexual sins such as relations with a married woman, incest, relations during menstruation and bestiality. The author has summarized these as a prohibition against the abuse of women (including the abuse of their status and honor). Women who freely choose to engage in any of these activities are also considered guilty under Jewish law.

Four of the Noahide laws are involved in creating a JUST society, controlled by the rule of law and focused on the prevention of crime. One of the laws is against cruelty, in other words, for the promotion of RESPECT and KINDNESS. The two final Noahide laws are in the domain of RELIGION.

So let's consider what would happen if everyone in the world were to sign up to these three concepts – Justice, Kindness, and Religion. What impact would it have on world peace?

2. Jews are permitted to eat meat from a kosher animal that has been killed through the act of *Shechita*. Non-Jews are permitted to eat from any animal that has been killed in any way. The only condition is that it must be dead at the time of eating. Pulling off a leg from a live dog to eat it is an act of cruelty that should not be tolerated in any society.

Chapter 18

A. JUSTICE LEADS TO PEACE

Firstly, JUSTICE.

If we went back in history some 5,000 years, we would find a very different type of life to the one we have today. People didn't live in large cities, not even in towns, but in small villages scattered around the countryside. Locations would have been selected because of their proximity to drinking water, food supplies, and/or security (for example at the top of a hill).

Men would have stood guard all night around their fenced village to protect women, children, and property from looters from neighboring towns. There would have been some villages that were more powerful, with stronger men and better weapons, and some villages that were more vulnerable.

If the food or water supply ran out, the village would not be able to depend on the generosity of neighboring villages – perhaps they would have to surrender all their belongings to the neighboring village, or wage war with an uncertain outcome.

Anyone wandering around at night alone would be subject to attack – mugging and probable death. Life would have been a game of survival, with all the time that one wasn't foraging for food spent defending oneself from outsiders.

In the words of Thomas Hobbes, the 17th century British philosopher,

> *Life was short, nasty and brutish*   (Leviathan, 1651)

And then came the rule of law. As villages grew to become towns, the economy of scale meant that some men could be paid to be full-time guards, leaders, and policemen. A ruling class arose that collected taxes (often penal ones), but the side benefit was a society that had some order. Thieves would be treated harshly by the local government and the quality of life, if not the average income, began to rise[1].

A society that abides by the rule of law is a far more pleasant society to live in than an anarchy and it increases peacefulness in the following ways:

i) At a basic level, punishments for theft and murder are a deterrent to potential criminals.

ii) Criminals are less likely to materialize from societies that are just, than from anarchies. And they are less likely to garner support from others in a lawful society.

iii) A town that has a system of justice to prosecute its own felons, is more likely to link up with friendly neighbors in order to combat aggressive neighbors. This is likely to spread the concept of justice further afield.

Overall, countries that have a just system of law are less likely to precipitate wars against other nations. And so the prevalence of just and fair legal systems is a major contributor to world peace.

However, justice is not enough to ensure peace. In history there are numerous examples of nations that committed crimes against humanity within their own definition of "law." Nazi Germany even enacted laws to justify the genocide of Jews within the framework of their legislature.

---

1. A fuller description of the anthropology of civilization can be found in "Guns, Germs and Steel," J Diamond, 1997, Norton.

Chapter 19

B. RESPECT LEADS TO PEACE

So peace requires more than purely justice. Peace requires respect and kindness.

The second category of the Noahide laws is RESPECT – exemplified by the command not to tear a limb off a live animal.

In society there are many important relationships. The most obvious relationship is that between humans. But there is also our relationship with animals and inanimate objects.

Humans have farmed animals and crops for thousands of years. Without a sensitivity to the needs of the plants and animals, this would not be possible. Plants need light, water, and minerals. A society that doesn't have a way of feeding its crops, or leaving the fields fallow every so many years, will eventually go without food. A society that mistreats its animals, depriving them of food, water or shade will find itself hungry when the animals die.

And so, as much as the quality of our lives depends upon our relationships with those around us, it also depends on our relationship with our environment. If we invested solely in our own comforts and ignored the resources around us, we would lose out in the end.

So the respectful treatment of plants, animals, and the environment is critical for our survival on this planet.

But the importance of this particular law also impacts on Peace.

It is possible for a society to be based on the strong rule of law, and yet for aggression to be an acceptable trait within that society. There are countless examples in distant and recent history of cruelty built into otherwise civilized societies. We can think about cruel sports – bull fighting, chicken baiting, dog fights, fox hunting and more. We can consider the mighty Roman Empire that threw early Christians to the lions in front of a Coliseum of spectators. We can think back to the slave trade in the USA and Europe, perpetrated by civil societies with judges, policemen, prisons, and reams of legal precedents.

So a legal system alone does not rule out cruelty. Sometimes cruelty may even be enshrined into misinformed legislatures.

The Noahide laws, however, forbid cruelty to animals. And therefore, by logic, even more so towards other humans. Cruel behavior may not be illegal in many secular legislatures, but in the Torah domain it is a denial of God's involvement in Creation.

A society where cruelty is allowed to fester breeds people who are violent and more likely to wage war. One can only imagine the sorts of influences that led to the creation of an Adolf Hitler. Reducing cruelty increases peace in society.

But respect and justice are not enough to create a peaceful world. There are many examples of societies where respect and justice are demonstrated within a population, but not towards other nations or even to minorities within their borders. In recent years we have seen tragedies in Serbia, Darfur, and Somalia where respect and justice has not been applied to those of other faiths or beliefs.

In order to achieve worldwide peace, we need more than justice and respect. We also need tolerance.

In the Noahide Laws, tolerance is mandated through religion.

Chapter 20

C. RELIGION BRINGS TOLERANCE AND PEACE

And we could ask, does religion really create tolerance and peace in the world?

Isn't religion the major cause of war and intolerance around the globe?!

And the answer is, "No! Well, not TRUE religion."

What is "true religion?"

The answer is given by our Rabbis, who describe a future time of peace.

According to their opinion,

> In the world to come, the righteous will dance around God in a circle. God will be in the middle. (Babylonian Talmud Taanit 31a)

This is the Jewish model of Monotheism – belief in one God.

So what is the message here?

I think it is threefold.

i) EQUALITY

The unique property of a circle over any other shape is that, geometrically, it is the only shape that has its middle equidistant from every point on its circumference. All the righteous are equidistant from God, who is in the center. Meaning that each and every person (Jew and non-Jew alike) is EQUAL in the eyes of God (so long as they live a "good" life and are, therefore, "righteous").

God in the center of the circle.

ii) RESPONSIBILITY

Anyone who has danced at a Jewish wedding, in a circle, will testify that you have to hold on tight. If one person lets go, and you're travelling at speed, then the whole circle falls apart. The imagery here seems to be that everyone in the circle is RESPONSIBLE for everyone else, to keep them in the group.

iii) GOD-CENTERED

God is in the middle. This is the ultimate message of the imagery. If God is in the middle of the circle, then God is the most important thing in the lives of everyone around the circle. Everyone is aspiring to be like God, not like one another. Nothing is more important than God in this image. We'll return to this idea in a moment, but this is the most critical concept.

Now, if people don't hold by Monotheism – the idea of One God – there are only two other possibilities – either they believe in NO god, or they believe in MULTIPLE gods. (Apologies to Mathematicians as I have ignored the possibility that they believe in a negative God or a fraction of God!)

So let's think about these two other possibilities.

THE NO GOD THEORY – ATHEISM

There are plenty of people in the world who call themselves Atheists. That is, they believe that there is no God.

What exactly does this mean?

It means that they do not believe that there is a Divine force in the Universe that cares how we act. There may be "Morality," but it is not something we learn from an external source, it is learned from an internal feeling.

In other words, in the absence of an external source, the Atheist defines what is right (and wrong) FOR HIM OR HERSELF.

And so, whereas Monotheism has God in the middle and all the righteous of mankind dancing around Him in a circle, Atheism has the SELF in the middle. Anyone like ME is, by definition, righteous. Anyone else is inferior. In Atheism, the righteous person is defined by ME.

It is fair to say that many people who classify themselves as Atheist may not actually be Atheist. Many Atheists are prepared to admit that there is an "external good," just that they don't believe in any definable God. Importantly, the Noahide laws do not require a specific understanding of who God is, just that such a Force exists, and hence these Atheists may well qualify as Monotheists from a Jewish standpoint.

THE MULTIPLE GOD THEORY

The final option for religion is idolatry – belief in multiple gods.

On the face of it, it is not obvious why such a belief is that different from belief in One God.

But consider the following scenario. On Sunday I bring a gift to the Sun god's idol because it is the beginning of the week and I want good weather to gather in my crops. On Wednesday I bring a gift to the idol of commerce, because I am busy selling my crops and want the best price. On Friday I worship the god of love because the weekend is approaching and I want success in my love life.

In this scenario, who is in the middle of my circle?

Who determines right and wrong, good and bad?

I might say, "the idol." But that would not be true. In fact, just as in the Atheist case above, the real center of my circle is . . . ME! Because it is ME who chooses which god to worship each day, depending on my needs and my mood. In the idolatrous world there is no overriding Divine power in the Universe that has to be constantly served. There are only my needs. Anyone who has similar needs to me is "righteous" in my eyes (at least today) and anyone who has differing needs is "evil" in my eyes (consider someone who wants low prices on a Wednesday because they are buying my crops!).

Again, it is very possible that non-Jews who worship "idols" today are not idolatrous according to this Torah definition. If they believe in a central Force that connects humanity and they "worship" statues out of habit, they may also be Monotheists in its broadest meaning.

ONE GOD

So when the Torah commands the whole of humanity with two specific laws regarding Religion, they are there to ensure that we put GOD in the middle of our circle.

And we can also understand why there must be two laws in this category:

i) Do not worship idols

ii) Do not curse God

because this model of "religion," which is that of true Monotheism, requires two separate acts of acknowledgement.

Firstly, we must discard the idea of putting ourselves at the center of our own circles, judging others by our own standards rather than by an external and pre-defined law. Hence "no idols."

And secondly we must put the One God firmly in the middle of our circle, understanding that there is Something greater than us that relates to all of humanity in an equal way. We are no more, or less, important than any other good person – just part of a huge macrocosm that depends on us pulling our weight and in the same direction (towards good).

Interestingly, one could ask why this second commandment is worded in the negative and not the positive. Why doesn't the Torah command mankind to believe in "God," why just command mankind not to "curse God." Here, the universal aspect of Judaism can be seen with clarity.

Non-Jews are not commanded to have the same understanding of God as Jews. Different religions are entitled to describe God in their own terms. After all, none of us, alive today, have seen Him personally and any descriptive words are insufficient to describe God[1].

But it is necessary not to *deny* the existence of the single God, even if we don't know precisely how to *describe* Him.

This "circle model" of God is, perhaps, our best understanding of God.

God is whatever is in the middle of our lives, more important than anyone else, loving us equally with others, and such that the whole of civilized society depends on the acceptance of His being there.[2]

Now, clearly, if universally accepted, this understanding of God would contribute hugely to Global Peace. If each culture did not consider *itself* in the middle of its circle, superior to everyone else on the periphery, but realized that there is Something much greater than all of us in the middle, that would pull us all together. With this simple understanding of God, we would surely have a chance, within humanity, for peaceful coexistence.

This also reveals the fallacy of the term "religious war." Any group that claims to be waging a religious war, or fighting for their "God," is, by definition, not doing so. Such a group is not putting God in the middle of their circle, but themselves. "Religions" that insist on

---

1. In fact that is why the Hebrew term used most commonly for God is "Hashem" – the "Name." While there are numerous more descriptive names used for God in the Torah, each of them focuses on only one small aspect of God's nature and not His totality. Hence the term "Hashem" which doesn't try to put God in a box.
2. He is also the Intelligent Being that created us and all the laws of morality (i.e., the Torah).

converting others, or treating those of other faiths as inferior, are, in reality, cults of the "self" and not religions based on any sophisticated understanding of God.

Tolerance is an essential feature of a true belief in God.

And this concept of tolerance goes right through the Torah, from the moment that man is created. In the words of the Rabbis:

> "Humanity was created from one person alone for the sake of peace, so that no one could say to another, 'My ancestor is greater than yours!'"   (Babylonian Talmud Sanhedrin 37a)

In summary, the seven Noahide laws, which fall into three categories – JUSTICE, RESPECT, AND RELIGION – are the basis for creating peace in the world. The purpose of Jews on this planet is to bring these universal laws to everyone. And Jews have, to a great extent, been successful in spreading these ideas to nations across the civilized world, as we will discuss.

Chapter 21

HOW DO JEWS CHANGE THE WORLD?

So how did the 0.2% of Jews in the world have such a huge impact on the 99.8% of the planet that they have, mostly, never encountered?

And how do we continue to do so?

And the answer is: through the most sophisticated system of inspiration, motivation, and training that has ever been devised.

And that system is the 613 commandments.

But how do the commandments achieve this massive impact on the world?

And here we must analyze the mitzvot to find out.

THE MITZVOT FALL INTO SIX GROUPS

According to the great 19th century Rabbi, Samson Rafael Hirsch of Frankfurt, the mitzvot fall into six distinct groups[1].

Group of Mitzvot	Examples
1. **Teachings** – Ideas & Behavior	Knowing that there is only one God, engaging in Torah learning, being humble and controlling one's animal soul
2. **Laws** – Civil and Criminal	Don't murder, steal, defraud or overcharge

---

1. *Nineteen Letters*, Feldheim.

Group of Mitzvot	Examples
3. **Respect** – for non-human life	Being sensitive to animals – not mixing milk and meat, slaughtering humanely, not wasting food sources, respecting the dead.
4. **Acts of Kindness**	Charity, helping the poor, sick, elderly, uneducated. Getting married, raising children, and educating them in a stable home.
5. **Prayer**	Prayer, blessings, public reading of the Torah. Also repentance and gratitude.
6. **Rituals**	Festivals, Shabbat, tefillin, prayer shawl, donations to the priestly caste, priestly blessing, and the Sabbatical year

The first thing to notice about this classification of mitzvot is that the Seven Noahide Laws fall into only three of these six categories: **Teachings, Respect,** and **Civil/Criminal Laws**.

i) The laws that legislate against idolatry and cursing God both fall into the category of **Teachings**, i.e., ideas and behavior.

ii) The four Noahide laws dealing with setting up courts of law, not murdering, stealing, or committing crimes against women – these all fall into the category of **Civil/Criminal Laws**.

iii) The final Noahide law, the one that prohibits the cutting off of limbs from living animals, falls into the category of **Respect** – laws that respect non-human life.

So the categories of **Teachings, Civil/Criminal Laws,** and **Respect** turn out to be universal categories.

These are the categories that directly bring peace to the world, as we have discussed above, and Jews and non-Jews together are responsible to keep these laws in order to achieve peaceful coexistence.

EXTRA LAWS FOR JEWS

"All of the Torah was given for the sake of promoting peace, as it says (Proverbs 3:17), 'Its ways are ways of pleasantness and all its paths are peace.'" (Babylonian Talmud Gittin 59a)

While there are only seven laws in the Torah that apply to the whole of humanity, there are (at least) another 606 that ONLY apply to Jews.

Why?

These "extra" laws fall into four categories:

i) Those "extra" laws within the three universal groups, **Teachings**, **Respect,** and **Civil/Criminal Laws**, but which are only incumbent on Jews.

And the "extra" laws that comprise the whole of the three "Jewish" categories of:

ii) **Acts of Kindness,**

iii) **Rituals,** and

iv) **Prayer.**

EXTRA TEACHINGS, RESPECT, AND CIVIL/CRIMINAL LAWS

If all of humanity is commanded to keep the basic laws of **Teachings** (religion), **Civil/Criminal Laws** (law and order), and **Respect** (kindness to non-human life) – then why are there extra laws in these categories that just apply to Jews?

Let's consider the category, **Respect**, laws that demand respect for non-human life.

Chapter 23

MORE RESPECT –
FOR NON-HUMAN LIFE

While non-Jews are given a most important law in this category – not to tear the limb off a living animal – Jews are commanded even further. Jews are commanded the whole gamut of keeping kosher. Keeping kosher comprises many individual laws, but principally it divides into three areas:

i) A restrictive list of animals that may and may not be eaten,

ii) Kosher slaughter,

iii) Separation of milk and meat.

If, from the perspective of peace, the purpose of all the laws of **Respect** is to create a kind personality through the medium of respecting animals and non-human life, then how do these complex and burdensome laws impact Jews, and ultimately non-Jews?

Let's consider the rules of keeping kosher under this lens

i) Animal selection

    a. Cows, deer, sheep, and goats are kosher.
       i. Horses, bears, camels, and pigs are not.

    b. Trout, salmon, bream, and carp are kosher.
       i. Sharks, whales, octopi, and shrimp are not.

    c. Chickens, pigeons, ducks, and geese are kosher.
       i. Eagles, hawks, pelicans, and storks are not.

Kosher mammals are easily farmed, docile animals that can be kept contained without significant maintenance as they build their body weight ready for slaughter. Non-kosher mammals – horses, camels, bears, and pigs are less docile in captivity and/or require more human involvement in looking after them. Out of these animals, the only animal frequently farmed for its meat, which is not kosher, is the pig. Pigs, being naturally omnivorous, have sharp canines and/or tusks which can cause major injury to other pigs in captivity. Hence breeding pigs are often kept in individual cages throughout their pregnancy and piglets often have to have their teeth sanded down (without anaesthetic) in order to prevent injury to other animals.

Kosher birds are either mostly land-bound – chickens, ducks, and geese – or easily contained – such as pigeons that were historically bred for communications by the Romans and lived in dovecotes. Birds that would not easily stay in confinement are not kosher.

Kosher fish are farmed with the least effort, historically with nets. Species which would be cruel, and complex, to contain, such as sharks and whales, are not kosher. Octopi and shrimp are less efficient to farm.[1]

The laws of animal selection can be seen as a way of minimizing the pain of farming or hunting, both for the animal and the hunter.

These laws put a burden of kindness onto Jews that is not required of non-Jews, but sets an example to others of the importance of animal welfare.

ii) Kosher Slaughter

Kosher slaughter requires the skills of a trained slaughterer and a super-sharp knife. The slaughterer is trained in the precise methods of cutting the windpipe and aorta in one quick movement. The knife must have no "nicks" in it and is sharpened regularly throughout the hours of work of the slaughterer.

If one compares this method with other methods of slaughter for, say, chickens, it is demonstrably more humane (although much more expensive).

In many commercial, non-kosher, abattoirs the chickens are "pre-stunned." They are connected onto a conveyor belt by their legs, hanging upside down in a long chain, and then dipped, head-first, into electrified water where they are simultaneously electrocuted

---

1. See   http://www.slowfood.com/slowfish/pagine/eng/pagina.lasso?-id_pg=87 which describes the problems with shrimp farming, especially the huge degree of bycatch. Bycatch is the catching of unwanted species at the same time as the farmed produce.

and drowned. This method, however, fails to kill all the chickens in the line and some percentage will go onto the next stage of the process (plucking and even mincing) while still conscious. Some experts[2] estimate that pre-stunning fails in as many as 10% of animals, leading to millions of animals suffering needlessly due to "modern" slaughter techniques.

The kosher method of slaughter is expensive due to the cost of a highly trained, religious slaughterer, and the need for each slaughter to be performed manually and individually. But the benefit is a near 100% success rate and a swift and painless procedure for the animal. Jews pay more for their meat to have it humanely slaughtered.

Kosher slaughter is a costly overhead that has been placed on Jews, but not on non-Jews. It demonstrates the importance of kindness, as a trait, towards animals and humans, and ultimately serves as an inspiration to others.

iii) Non-mixing of milk and meat

Milk is the food that a young animal drinks from its mother's teats. Meat is the dead flesh – often of a young, tender animal. To eat milk and meat together, or even to see them cooking together, should awaken in us a sense of sadness for the young animal. The very animal that should have been consuming that milk is now sitting, cooked in it, on our plate.

Jews don't just refrain from eating and cooking[3] milk and meat together, for this reason, but also refrain from using cooking utensils, dishes, and cutlery for both milk and meat.

This, again, is a costly overhead for a Jewish family – requiring them to own two sets of cutlery, dishes and pots and pans. But it instills a deep sense of compassion for animal and human life that spreads to many other parts of human experience.

A people whose role is to spread the Noahide laws across the world, including the law against cruelty to animals, must surely demonstrate a higher adherence to these values than those on whom they make their impression.

2. See "Dutch vote to ban religious slaughter of animals" Reuters, Ivana Sekularac, 28/6/11

3. Jews are also commanded not to sell products that contain a kosher animal's meat cooked in a kosher animal's milk.

Chapter 24

RESPECT – FOR THE DEAD

The laws of **Respect** also extend to how we treat our dead. When a loved one passes away, there is a precise procedure that must be undertaken.

The limbs of the deceased are straightened and his/her jaw is closed, in order that the body is in a dignified position before rigor mortis sets in. The body is then covered with a sheet and the body is not left unattended until the burial team arrives. The Jewish burial team (the *chevra kaddisha*) takes the body and washes it thoroughly. Then they dress it in a plain white cotton gown and place it in a simple wooden casket with wooden pegs (no metal nails).

The simplicity of the burial is key to the concept of **Respect**. The Rabbis decreed that every Jew should have a respectful burial. In order to ensure that poorer Jews did not have a lesser experience, they decreed that every Jew should have the simplest burial.

The message is strong and clear. In life we may choose to believe that we are different in importance to others, but in death, we are all clearly equals.

The extra laws in the category of **Respect** ensure that Jews better understand the importance of Nature and the equality of humanity, imperatives if we are to share these ideas with the world.

Chapter 25

EXTRA LAW AND ORDER

What about the group of laws known as **Civil/Criminal Laws**? Law and order?

Why do Jews need more of these than non-Jews?

Jews have more than the four Noahide laws in this class which are not to murder, steal, nor commit sexual crimes, and to set up courts of law.

Indeed, these extra laws appear to work, as the crime level in Israel is around 50% that of the UK or America based on a recent worldwide comparison.[1]

For Jews, the **Civil/Criminal Laws** also include rules on workers rights, not overcharging (or underpaying), laws against charging interest to fellow Jews, and much more.

What are the details of these extra laws?

i) Workers' rights

These include the right to be paid on time: a daily worker must be paid by the end of the day; a weekly worker by the end of the week; and a monthly worker by the end of the month.

ii) One is not allowed to overcharge or underpay

Indeed, for certain commodity food items, the limit is explicitly set at 20%. Above this level of overcharging one has the right to reverse the transaction. If one underpaid for an item, the shopkeeper has the right to reverse the transaction too.

---

1. See http://en.wikipedia.org/wiki/List_of_countries_by_intentional_homicide_ rate which shows a homicide rate of 1.8 crimes per 100,000 inhabitants in Israel versus 4.7 in the USA.

iii) Not charging interest to fellow Jews

The laws prohibiting interest to fellow Jews, but not to non-Jews, are well known. They led to Jews becoming the money-lenders of Europe in the Middle Ages when Christians and Muslims were forbidden by their religions to lend to one another.

From a cynical perspective one might easily suggest that the law of only charging interest to non-Jews is a racist law. Perhaps God in His wisdom wanted to protect Jews from the whims of Jewish money lenders but He was not so concerned about non-Jews being forced to pay back loans with usurious levels of interest.

However, this is not the case as is clear from the analysis of our Rabbis. A Jew whose greatest resource is his skill set – such as a builder, a doctor, or a lawyer – is permitted to charge Jews for his time (his greatest asset). So why should a Jew with money not be allowed to charge other Jews for the use of his assets? Certainly a land owner is permitted to charge rent for the use of his property – so why should the lending of money be any different?

We can only speculate as to the reason for these laws, but certainly the laws against charging interest have created many new and innovative forms of finance – perhaps most notably the institution of Private Equity or Venture Capital.

By Jewish law, one is not allowed to lend $1,000 to someone to help them in their business and to charge 10% interest per annum on the loan. But one would be perfectly free to invest $1,000 in their business for an appropriate percentage of the ownership (5%, 10%, even more) and to collect the percentage of profit associated with the investment (which could yield much more that 10% of the original investment per annum).

Why?

A plausible answer would be – it's all about alignment of interests.

If I lend $1,000 to someone and expect it to be paid back in three years with interest, and I secure the loan against their home or car, then I have no risk, just the upside when the money comes back to me. If his business suffers, I don't care, from a financial standpoint, because my loan and profit is guaranteed. So I may make the appropriate noises expressing sympathy with his difficult situation, but at the end of the day, I know I will collect.

If, however, I have a share in his business, then our interests are fully aligned. If he succeeds, I prosper. If he fails, I lose. Now, when he asks for my help in his business, I am inclined to do what I can to make him succeed.

A community thrives when its members understand that the success of one of its members builds prosperity for all. A community collapses when everyone is out for themselves and themselves alone.

The requirement to lend money without interest (or as equity) builds a strong community. But it is unreasonable to legislate these rules outside the community. Part of being in a community also gives the borrower a moral requirement to pay back on a loan. Microloans in Africa work exactly on this principle. Small groups of (mainly) women are given small loans to pay for a cow or a sewing machine. They are tasked with paying back the loan over a reasonable time. Regular meetings with the group ensure that the moral pressure to repay the loan is understood and the repayment rates are so spectacular, that this has become a multi-billion dollar industry in recent years.

Outside the community, this moral pressure does not exist. If there were a prohibition against lending money on interest to foreigners, that would just restrict the circulation of money and would be bad for the economy of Jews and non-Jews.

Modern governments frequently implement special lending vehicles just for their own citizens that make house buying cheaper and safer, while not offering such deals to foreign buyers. This is understood to be good for civil society. Modern governments recognize that they don't have the same moral responsibility to enable non-citizens to buy their homes.

There are also tangible benefits to non-Jews from the level of trust that exists between Jews in the field of business.

A great example of the power of trust within a culture is the Antwerp diamond market. This market, operating as the main diamond bourse in Europe for the past few hundred years, is dominated by Orthodox Jews. The main costs in creating a diamond market are twofold: security (and/or insurance for the diamonds that can cost $100,000s) and legal contracts (when diamonds are taken on sale or return – and their return must be guaranteed). In the Orthodox community in Antwerp, the level of trust between the market makers is such that security and legal costs are minimized. Part of the reason for this is that if one party were to defraud another their position within the community would be at stake – it would affect their children's ability to marry within the community.

The diamond industry is a good example of the importance of close community. And it benefits not just the Jewish community, but the wider world, which can purchase diamonds at a lower cost because of the level of trust that exists between Jewish intermediaries.

Overall the **Civil/Criminal Laws**, which are legislated only for Jews, help to cement a Jewish community that serves as an example to the world in business ethics and crime control. All very important if the Jews have a responsibility to promote justice and ethical conduct for the sake of greater world peace.

Chapter 26

EXTRA TEACHINGS –
MORE RELIGIOUS IDEALS

Jews also have more laws in the category of **Teachings** than non-Jews.

The Noahide laws proscribe two **Teachings** regarding religious belief and conduct:

i) The prohibition of worshipping idols

ii) The prohibition of cursing the One God – Hashem

As has been explained above, the person who understands these two concepts puts God in the middle of his/her circle and not him/herself. And that person understands that every (good) human being has a direct and equal link to God and that he/she has no superiority over others.

For Jews, however, there are more **Teachings** which include Torah learning, and the ideals of humbling oneself and controlling one's desires.

Why are these important for the Jew as change agent in society?

1. Torah study

The Torah is the book that drives all Jewish action. The Torah contains the 613 mitzvot and is the instruction manual for Jewish life. Therefore it is incumbent on every Jew to study the Torah.

Interestingly, the Rabbis discuss the minimum requirement for Torah study each day and they agree that it is the recital of one verse in the Torah, *Devarim* 6:4, which reads "Listen Israel, the Lord your God, the Lord is One."

The famous commentator, Rashi, explains this verse. The concept of one God is not a simple one. As we discussed already in Chapter

19, Monotheism is qualitatively different from Idolatry and Atheism. Monotheism is about putting God in the middle of your circle and understanding that all of mankind is equidistant from God, on the circumference of that circle, ALONG with YOU.

So how does Rashi, the famous French commentator of the 11th century, explain this verse that is so important? How does he explain this verse that is the first that a Jewish child learns to say, that is said at least twice a day in our prayer services (the *Shema*), and on waking and going to sleep? Rashi explains that it means "Listen Jewish people to this message – 'your concept of God will be the universal understanding of God in the time to come.'"

To Rashi, the *Shema* is not so much a statement of belief, but a MISSION statement for the whole Jewish people – to spread an understanding of Monotheism across humanity. And what will be the result of this global acknowledgement of a common Creator Who connects all of mankind? World peace!

And we see this in the Talmud. There is a famous, and shocking, story of Rabbi Akiva who is skinned alive by the Romans with a hot comb in front of his students.

> *Rabbi Akiva shouts out "Listen Israel, the Lord our God, the Lord is One" as he is being tortured to death. One of his students shouts out "Even to this extent?!" To which Rabbi Akiva answers, "All my life I have wanted to fulfill this verse 'with all my life,' even when they take your life, and now I can!" He then dies, reciting "Shema Yisrael."*
>
> (Babylonian Talmud Brachot 61b)

What does this story mean? Rabbi Akiva understands that the verse "Listen Israel" means that a Jew's task is to bring the message of Monotheism to the non-Jewish world. His student asks "Even to this extent?!" – meaning, "How can you pray for the acceptance of God by the non-Jews when they are taking your life? Do you really care about their welfare at this point?!" To which Rabbi Akiva answers, "Yes! We are commanded to say the Shema with all our soul – meaning even when others are persecuting us and killing us. Now I can fulfill this verse in its fullest meaning!"

Another reminder of the meaning of this verse is in the Shabbat morning service, where the *Shema* is recited an extra time during the additional service, in the repetition of the *Amida*. Why is it recited at that point? Answer our Rabbis – a Persian King in the 5th century prohibited the recital of the *Shema* in public, and he policed synagogues during the morning service when it was publically recited. Since the guards left before the additional service, the Rabbis inserted this critical verse into the liturgy there.

Why did the King forbid this particular verse and no other? Now, if it were purely because of its cry for Monotheism then there are plenty of Psalms and other prayers which would have to be removed. Apparently this Persian King understood the verse to be a Mission statement for the Jewish people to "convert" non-Jews to Judaism (as we have seen this is not the case at all, just a call for Global Monotheism) – and so he banned its recital.

2. Humility

> One of the commandments in the Torah is for a Jew to be humble.
> The Torah describes Moses as "the most humble person in the
> world."   (Bamidbar 12:3)

The Mishnah, Ethics of the Fathers, goes further and says that there are three defining features of a Jew:

> Mercy, Humility and Kindness.   (Babylonian Talmud Yevamot 79a)

Clearly, humility is a goal to aspire to. But why?

Say our Rabbis –

> God says about the arrogant "he and I cannot be in the same room!"
>   (Babylonian Talmud Erachin 15b)

What does this mean?

It means that if I am so big-headed to believe that my achievements and successes are all from within myself then I cannot, simultaneously, believe in a Creator who gave them to me as His blessings. In other words, if I am arrogant I cannot truly accept the concept of Monotheism, i.e., God being in the middle of my circle.

So humility is the result of fully recognizing the existence of the One God.

3. Controlling our desires

One of the strong themes that we can pick up from the Torah is the requirement to control our desires. And these desires are animal desires.

From the opening chapter of *Bereishit* and the introduction of Adam and Eve in the Garden of Eden, the message is clear – don't behave like a reptile, like the snake that tempted Eve with the apple.[1] Instead, control that passion and direct it to higher purposes.

Interestingly, the ideal is not to quash passion, but just to redirect it. Passion is a great asset, so much so that our Rabbis explained:

> *No man has a strong will to do good who doesn't also have a strong will to do bad.*
> (Bereishit Rabba 9:9)

Destroying passion (which can be achieved by an aesthetic lifestyle – away from temptations and many sources of joy) is not a Jewish concept. Rather, the Torah commands a channelling of passion into worthy pursuits.

In the words of our Rabbis:

> *When we come to present ourselves at the heavenly gates we will be asked "Did you engage in all permissible pleasures?" And we will be punished for those we didn't partake of.*
> (Jerusalem Talmud Kedushin Chapter 4)

Animal passions can, however, flare up when, for example, food, sex or money are at stake. The Torah doesn't stigmatize these things, but rather forces us to channel our energies into productive and spiritual areas when engaging in them.

Food must be consumed with a blessing that recognizes God's creation. Sex must be within the confines of a loving marriage, and only at set times in the month that show respect to the woman. And

---

1. In fact our Rabbis explain that the fruit was not an apple – it was either a pomegranate, a fig or a bunch of grapes – all of which are fruits that emanate from Israel and the Fertile Crescent. Equally, the Rabbis saw in the snake imagery a phallic reference, apparently the snake didn't necessarily just want to feed Eve . . .

money may be accumulated so long as a percentage (ranging from 10%–20%[2]) of one's income is given annually to charity.

Controlling one's desires is essential for a people who are to make an impression on the world through their lifestyle. It also helps to abolish the "me" and create the "we" that is essential for a flourishing community and society.

So, as with the categories of **Civil/Criminal Law** and **Respect**, Jews are commanded to engage in **Teachings**, over and above that of the Noahide laws. In doing so, Jews create a community that is cohesive – a team that is fit to embark upon the task of transforming the world.

2. Why is there an upper limit on the amount of charity one is permitted to give? Answer our Rabbis – because a person must not make himself poor through giving charity. In other words, we have a responsibility to others, but also to ourselves. As with everything in life – charity is about balance.

Chapter 27

MIND, BODY, AND SOUL

So what about the remaining three categories of mitzvot that are not incumbent on non-Jews at all? What is their purpose in the scheme of transforming the world to a place of peace?

These three categories are specifically for the Jew as "change agent."

Say our Rabbis, we humans are made up of three components:

mind, soul, and body.

And these next three categories of laws enable us to mobilize each component.

i) PRAYERS – activate the mind

ii) RITUALS – activate the soul

iii) ACTS OF KINDNESS – activate the body

Interestingly, the three groups of laws that we share with non-Jews also relate to mind, body, and soul:

iv) TEACHINGS – beliefs and behaviors – the domain of the mind

v) RESPECT – prevention of cruelty – the domain of the soul

vi) CIVIL/CRIMINAL LAWS – the domain of the body

The latter group, the Universal laws, are predominantly about constraint – e.g., withholding oneself from idol worship, avoidance of cruelty, and prevention of crime. Whereas, the former three categories of law, those specifically for Jews, are predominantly about creating positive energy in the mind, body, and soul – praying for the right things, ritualizing important values, and behaving in an exceptional manner.

Six categories of law	Mind	Soul	Body
Universal laws (restraint) (commanded to Jews and non-Jews)	TEACHINGS (Religion)	RESPECT (to non-human life)	CIVIL and CRIMINAL LAW
Particularistic laws (motivation) (commanded only to Jews)	PRAYER	RITUALS	ACTS OF KINDNESS

Only a people that has been fully motivated by positive energy can perform the task of change agent in difficult circumstances (often through major times of persecution) over multiple generations.

So how does this process of energization work?

Chapter 28

ACTIVATING THE MIND – PRAYER

If one were to count all the mitzvot in the Torah, the largest group of them would be **Prayer** (accounting for around a third of all the mitzvot). These include the laws of sacrifices, priests, Temple up-keep and so on. Today, without an operational Temple in Jerusalem, we are left with one major category of religious worship and that is **PRAYER**.

What is prayer? It is an act of speech – in Jewish prayer one should hear oneself saying the words (quietly) rather than just read them in one's mind.

So who's listening? Who are the prayers for?

We might answer – "They're for God, of course!"

But, according to our Rabbis,

> *"God is perfect [complete] . . . and He is not affected by anything."*
> (Rambam, "Thirteen Articles of Faith")

So who does need our prayers? A hint to the answer is in the He-brew word "to pray," which is *"Lehitpallel."* This is the reflexive form of the verb meaning to judge. So the Hebrew word "to pray" literally means "to stand in self judgement." So who is benefitting from my prayers? The answer is: "Me!"

I pray to God, yes! But the benefit of my prayers accrues to me. God doesn't need my prayers so much as I need to pray to Him.

So prayer is about affecting myself through thought.

I wake up in the morning and I am immediately subject to my body's needs and complaints:

- "Oh no, not another day of work"
- "What about the homework I haven't done?"
- "I'm hungry"
- "What about paying the bills?"
- "Where's the toilet?"

And my first intellectual encounter of the day will direct me to frame my thoughts one way or another.

For many people, the first intellectual encounter of the day is either through the news or through prayer.

Chapter 29

THE NEWS IS NOT REAL

The radio alarm, the newspaper, or an app may take us directly to the "news." But what is the "news?" We might think that it is a list of events that recently "happened" in the world, brought to us objectively by the world's press. But this is not the case.

"News" is whatever sells as "news."

– Few people are interested that the vast majority of pop stars are happily married with 2.4 children and a dog. But whenever a pop star splits up with his wife or eats his dog, that's "news."

– Few people are interested that most politicians go about their day to day jobs with care and a passion for their constituents. But if one politician takes a bribe on a specific occasion, that's "news."

– Few people are interested in the fact that most people in the world are civilized and considerate about others. But if one person commits a war crime, rape or burglary, that's "news."

News is whatever stirs us up. Unfortunately, this "news" stirs up our animalistic nature.

Newspapers are full of stories about sex, war, and money. They make us feel jealous, greedy and, very often, in a patronizing way, happy not to be afflicted in the way of the news victim. Fascinating, titillating, but not healthy for the soul.

When I finish reading a newspaper or watching a news program, I believe that the world is a place of sex and riches (of which I don't have enough) and violence (that I can't avoid). But this is not TRUE.

Chapter 30

TRUTH AND LIES

TRUTH, say our Rabbis, is about seeing the whole picture. The Hebrew word for TRUTH, *Emet*, אמת, consists of the first, middle, and last letters of the Hebrew alphabet. It also spells Mother -אמ and Death מת-. The Hebrew word for lie, *Sheker* שקר consists of three consecutive letters in the Hebrew alphabet. The letters of *Emet* are all letters that stand on two legs. The letters of *Sheker* are all letters that stand on one leg.

Say our Rabbis, the difference between truth and lies is that truth is seeing the whole picture – from beginning to end – from birth to death. And truth stands on two legs – it can be tested from multiple angles and it always stands up, and stands the test of time.

Lies are true to an extent, otherwise they'd just be stupid statements. But they're only a small part of the truth. They don't stand the test of time, nor do they stand up against investigation.

Newspapers contain some truths – much of what they say is verifiable. But they are not TRUE. They do not present the whole picture of life, just a small perspective – one that appeals to our lowest animal instincts.

The Rabbis tell us that:

> *Three things take us out of this world – jealousy, greed, and pride.*
> (Mishnah, Ethics of the Fathers 4:21)

The "news" activates these base instincts in us, but they are ultimately destructive feelings. They may titillate us in the short term, but they leave us feeling dissatisfied with our lot.

So what's the alternative? Prayer.

Chapter 31

THE ANTIDOTE TO "NEWS" IS PRAYER

Prayer is a gift from Hashem, and totally counterintuitive. Who would have thought that spending a short time, each morning and evening, reflecting about God could be beneficial to *us*?

Prayer in Judaism is threefold:

i) **Praise**: acknowledging God's creation of everything, especially the wonders of life

ii) **Requests**: asking[1] God for all the good things in life – including good health, sufficient funds, freedom, independence, and peace

iii) **Thanks**: showing gratitude to God for everything that happens to us, acknowledging it is all for the good even though we can't immediately see it that way

Prayer is the antithesis of the "news."

While the "news" makes us feel discontent with all that we have, prayer generates a feeling of contentment that we live in such a beautiful world. This is the power of PRAISE.

While the "news" leaves us wanting more money, sex, and power, prayer forces us to ask for good health, sufficient funds, love, and peace. This is the power of REQUESTS.

While the "news" generates in us feelings of jealousy, observing others that have more than us, or self-satisfaction against those far

---

1. Note: based on what we discussed above, that prayer is more for our benefit than God's, these requests can also be seen as benefitting us by putting the "right" sort of requests into our mouths.

less fortunate, prayer generates feelings of gratitude, appreciation, and a desire to help those in need. This is the power of THANKS.

Prayer is taking time out during a busy day to stop and appreciate how good life is. And this is so important in a world where the "news" is constantly telling us how brutal and unfair our lives are.

Chapter 32

THE BEGINNING
SHAPES OUR DAY

Recent psychological research has helped us understand some of the benefits of prayer. In a recent study, one group of students at a university was selected and asked to sit in a room and find words in a word search grid. The words that they were asked to select were mostly neutral words (e.g. "cat," "dog," "table," etc.) but also contained a small selection of "kind" words (e.g. "kind," "generous," "gift"). When they came out of their room, at the end of the allotted time, a young man was standing with a charity box at the end of the hallway. The amount of money donated by the group was noted.

In a control experiment, a similar number of students was selected and sat at the same exercise in the same room. But this time, along with the neutral words were words of "unkindness" (e.g. "stingy," "mean," "miserly"). This time, the same man stood in the corridor at the end of the allotted time with his charity box and the amount collected was noted.

What is fascinating is that the first group, with the "kind" words, gave substantially more that the second group with the "unkind" words.

In other words, even though the "kind" words were not even spoken as part of a moral lecture, the very fact that they were scanned by the eyes of the students (and in this case, circled on a grid) was sufficient to change their behavior for at least a few minutes into the day!

This is the impact of prayer. Even though we don't always think deeply about the meaning of the prayers, or even the words we say, our subconscious mind has been exposed to them – and that is enough to make a difference to our outlook on life and our behavior.

I remember hearing Clive Lawton, an accomplished Jewish educator, speaking about his trip to India as a student. He recalled how he had to sleep on a crowded train platform overnight in order to catch his early train. When he awoke, he wanted to put on his *tefillin* (prayer boxes) and *tallit* (prayer shawl) to pray. Conscious of all the Indian men and women around him, and anxious about how odd he would appear, tying black boxes onto his arm and head with black leather straps, he covered himself with his prayer shawl and put his *tefillin* on beneath it. And then he prayed.

When he finished, he quietly took off the *tefillin* and wrapped them up and put them away and folded his prayer shawl. Only then did he look around himself, expecting to see everyone's eyes upon him. How wrong he was! As his eyes scanned the hundreds of people awaking from their sleep on the platform, he noticed that every one of them had some sort of morning ritual, an idol and/or a prayer amulet, to worship their god. No one was paying the least bit of notice towards him, because in the Eastern world it is the most natural thing to pray to your god as you rise!

Only in our modern society have we decided, in general, to dispense with God and prayer. But we've substituted God and prayers with TV, radio, and the "news" – and instead of satisfaction we've bred discontent.

So PRAYER, worshiping God, is important to Jews as change agents, because it creates a positive outlook on life and a desire to help others from the moment we jump out of bed.

Chapter 33

FRAMING OUR DAYS
WITH PEACE

But there is another key reason that prayer is critical to the Jew as peacemaker. And this is expressed in the following Midrash:

"Great is peace for all blessings and prayers culminate with peace. The [Shabbat evening] blessings of 'Shema Yisrael' conclude with, 'Blessed are You God Who spreads over us the tent of PEACE*' [the weekday evening variant – not cited in the Midrash – says that God 'guards our coming and going for life and for* PEACE*']. The Amidah prayer concludes with, 'Blessed are You God Who blesses His people Israel with* PEACE*.' The blessing by the Kohanim concludes with, 'And may God grant you* PEACE*'" (Vayikra Raba, Tzav).*

One could add numerous more examples of prayers that end in peace, including the *Bentching* (Grace after Meals) prayer that ends "God blesses His people with PEACE" and the important Kaddish prayer, recited multiple times during each prayer service, that concludes with a request for PEACE.

So, the bottom line of Jewish prayer, and the final word, is PEACE.

Prayer is our mantra, repeated over and over again, to bring peace to the world.

Everything a Jew does in his or her life is, ultimately, for peace.

Our Rabbis also stated that the purpose of the mitzvot is to bring us closer to God or to a closer understanding of Him. If this sounds like a contradiction with the concept that one performs mitzvot for the sake of bringing peace to the world, then we must remember that one of God's names is "SHALOM," peace.

Chapter 34

GREAT IS REPENTANCE AS IT LEADS TO PEACE

Another commandment in the category of PRAYER, required by Jews, is repentance.

What is repentance, and does it, too, have a bearing on peace?

The Hebrew word for repentance, *teshuvah* gives us a clue as to the true purpose of repentance. *Teshuvah* is derived from the Hebrew word to "return."

Return to what?

There are different answers to this question:

i) Returning to our perfect state of childhood

    a. When we were unprejudiced – and we valued everyone who was kind to us equally

    b. When we were intrigued by everything – and we hadn't yet become so accustomed to things that we ignored them

    c. When we knew that God existed because it was obvious that there must be a Creator

ii) Or, perhaps, returning to the state of Adam and Eve in the Garden of Eden, in Paradise

    a. A time of innocence

    b. A time before we knew evil

    c. A time before negative attitudes existed

iii) Or, perhaps, just returning to our state before we erred

    In the words of our Rabbis:

Great is repentance as it leads to redemption   *(Babylonian Talmud*
  Yoma 86b)

Redemption – represents a state of global and personal peace. We will be ultimately redeemed in the Messianic period – that's global peace. And we are individually redeemed on an ongoing basis when we find inner peace – satisfaction and happiness. So repentance leads to both peace and happiness.

Chapter 35

THREE TIME FRAMES
OF HAPPINESS

Tal Ben-Shahar, former Harvard lecturer in positive psychology, made a breakthrough in the analysis of happiness when he segmented happiness into two time frames – past and present.1

Ben-Shahar recounts the time when he won the Israeli under-16 squash championships that he had been training for obsessively for four years. During his period of training, he had abstained from eating fast food hamburgers, his favorite meal, in order to maintain his optimum weight. Following the gold medal ceremony he rushed to the nearest fast food joint and stood at the counter to order his dinner.

He recalls how he felt a tension, standing there at the counter. Should he order a high fat burger which he knew would taste delicious, but be bad for his health in the long term? Or, should he choose a veggie burger which would taste like cardboard but probably be a healthier option?

This led him to develop his two dimensional model of happiness that became a winner at Harvard, bringing 800 students a week to his course, the most popular course in the university at the time!

Ben-Shahar explained that in our daily lives we often have to choose between happiness now, or happiness in the future. Sometimes we get neither. Sometimes we get both.

His two dimensional model yields four different burgers (that correspond to four different life choices):

---

1. "The Question of Happiness: On Finding Meaning, Pleasure, and the Ultimate Currency", Tal Ben Shahar, iUniverse, 2002

The **vegetarian burger** represents happiness in the future at the expense of happiness now. It corresponds to those who live "the rat race," working hard now in order to be able to retire early.

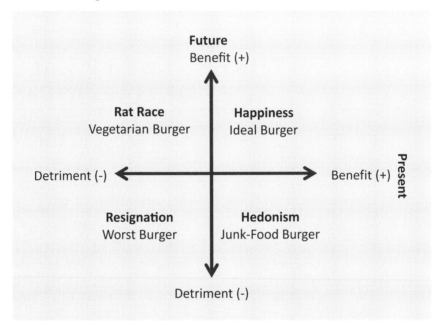

The **junk-food burger** represents happiness now at the expense of happiness in the future. It represents the hedonist lifestyle – living for the moment and not caring what tomorrow brings.

The **"worst burger"** is neither tasty nor good for you. It corresponds to a lifestyle that is not fun in the present and is unlikely to bring happiness in the future.

The **"ideal burger"** represents, of course, the elusive lifestyle that one enjoys now and that leads to even greater enjoyment in the future.

A great model of happiness and inspiration.

However, any two dimensional model always gets me thinking – as life is mostly three dimensional (past, present and future). So why didn't Ben-Shahar talk about happiness about the past?

Well, what is happiness "about the past"?

That's repentance!

We live our lives and we make mistakes. Sometimes we can forget them, but more often those mistakes nag at us and prevent us from being completely happy.

How can we achieve a state of happiness, or contentment, about our past mistakes? Through repentance!

Repentance is the ability to crystallize feelings of regret and anguish about our past mistakes, and resolve not to make the same mistakes again. After we go through the mental process of repentance, we feel cleansed. We can be happy about our past. We can even acknowledge that somehow we have grown from our mistakes. As the famous saying goes:

> *Good Judgment comes from Experience. Experience comes from Bad Judgment!*

Our Rabbis expressed this slightly differently:

> *"Great is repentance because it has the power to turn pre-meditated errors into merits!"*

How so? Because the self-analysis brought about by repentance can make me into a better person in the long run.

For example, if I was rude to someone in the office, and then felt really upset about it, those feelings of regret (i.e., *Teshuvah*), could lead me to being especially sensitive to the feelings of others in the future. I can become a better person through my mistakes.

But how does repentance also help to bring Global Peace?

Well, happy people are more inclined to help others (see the next chapter). People who are sad or depressed tend to turn inwards.

Repentance is an essential ingredient if one is to achieve contentment with one's past. And contentment with one's past is essential for someone who wishes to make a better future for others.

Chapter 36

HAPPY PEOPLE TRANSFORM THE WORLD

Psychologists have discovered a strong link between happiness and care for others.

The *Journal of Happiness Studies* recently published a study that revealed:[1]

> Participants . . . reported their level of happiness. Afterward, when they were asked to choose whether to spend a monetary windfall on themselves or someone else . . . **the happier participants felt, the more likely they were to choose to spend a windfall on someone else in the near future**.

Additionally, sociologists have discovered a strong link between religion and care for others OUTSIDE that religion. Robert Putnam, Professor of Public Policy at Harvard University, states the following:

> "Religions make Americans into better neighbors and better citizens . . . ethnic diversity has the opposite effect . . . Diversity seems to trigger not in-group / out-group division, but anomie or social isolation. In colloquial language, people living in ethnically diverse settings appear to "hunker down" – that is, to pull in like a turtle."[2]

So, religious practice, consisting of acts that make us happy [such as taking time off (Shabbat and festivals), getting married, being part of a community of similar minded people, getting educated

---

1. Source: "Happiness Runs in a Circular Motion: Evidence for a Positive Feedback Loop between Prosocial Spending and Happiness" from *Journal of Happiness Studies*, 2011.
2. "Bowling Alone," Robert Putnam, Simon & Shuster, 2001.

and helping others] is essential if we are to engage with the wider world and attempt to impact it for the better.

Overall, the category of PRAYER, worship, consisting of prayer and repentance, is an essential ingredient in personal happiness and leads to a more positive attitude towards helping others. Combined with the strong message of peace, stated and restated multiple times each day, Jewish prayer is the ultimate way to activate the mind towards building peace in the world.

Chapter 37

RITUALS –
CREATING THE FEELING

If prayer is the way to activate the mind towards the concept of changing the world and creating peace, then rituals are the way to activate the heart and soul.

Every Jewish ritual has a deep message, even though sometimes we perform the ritual without thinking about it. Often the message can only be absorbed by doing the act first and then experiencing the feelings derived from it. Rituals primarily impact the soul and not the mind.

Chapter 38

RITUALS – THINKING FAST, THINKING SLOW

Much has been written about the purpose and benefit of rituals and, most recently, even their dangers.

One of the most famous critics of religion, Richard Dawkins, wrote the following open letter to his daughter in which he openly criticizes the use of any technique that is not understood or completely rational:

To my dearest daughter,

Now that you are ten, I want to write to you about something that is important to me. Have you ever wondered how we know the things that we know? How do we know, for instance, that the stars, which look like tiny pinpricks in the sky, are really huge balls of fire like the Sun and very far away? And how do we know that the Earth is a smaller ball whirling round one of those stars, the Sun? The answer to these questions is 'evidence'. . . . Sometimes evidence means actually seeing (or hearing, feeling, smelling . . . .) that something is true . . .

A few months ago, I went on television to have a discussion with about 50 children. These children were invited because they'd been brought up in lots of different religions. Some had been brought up as Christians, others as Jews, Muslims, Hindus, Sikhs. The man with the microphone went from child to child, asking them what they believed. Their beliefs turned out to have no connection with evidence. They just trotted out the beliefs of their parents and grandparents, which, in turn, were not based upon evidence either. They said things like, 'We Hindus believe so and so.' 'We Muslims believe such and such.' 'We Christians believe something else.' Of course, since they all believed different things, they couldn't all be right . . .

What can we do about all this? It is not easy for you to do anything, because you are only ten. But you could try this. Next time somebody tells you something that sounds important, think to yourself: 'Is this the kind of thing that people probably know because of evidence? Or is it the kind of thing that people only believe because of tradition, authority or revelation?' And, next time somebody tells you that something is true, why not say to them: 'What kind of evidence is there for that?' And if they can't give you a good answer, I hope you'll think very carefully before you believe a word they say.

Your loving,
Daddy

Dawkins logic is very compelling. But it is *sheker*, only a small part of the truth, not *emet*, the whole truth. Every component of what he says is individually logical, but collectively it is wrong.

The best demonstration of this is from another scientist, a Nobel Prize winning scientist, Daniel Kahneman.

In his book, *Thinking, Fast and Slow*, Professor Daniel Kahneman explains that we humans are not, actually, rational beings who make decisions based on facts.

In an incredible analysis that won him the Nobel Prize for Economics in 2002 (despite him being a psychologist!), Kahneman shows how the vast majority of the thousands of decisions we make each day are impulsive and not deeply considered. What transpires from his work is that we have two decision-making systems in our brain – an impulsive one for fast decisions and a slower system for more complex decisions that takes more time and energy. Surprisingly, he demonstrates that the vast majority of decisions are made by the fast, non-rational, system!

In a recent television documentary about his work, he demonstrates this in a very compelling way, by choosing random people in a park to walk alongside of him. As they are walking, he asks them to count backwards from 100 in jumps of 8. After the first one or two answers, the candidate invariably stops walking to think more deeply. Kahneman explains that this is the slower system kicking into action. It requires more of our brain space and therefore prevents us from walking or doing other actions that also place a burden on our minds.

Given the thousands of decisions we make every day – when to get up, what to wear, how to travel to work or school – Kahneman demonstrates that it would be impossible for our rational system to be utilized more than in a small fraction of decisions. The vast majority of our life actually runs on auto-pilot!

Kahneman also demonstrates this with a test on pricing. He takes a random group of people and asks them to pick out a ball from a large bag with numbers between 1 and 100. After they pick out the ball, he hands them a bottle of wine and asks them how much they would pay for it. In the first iteration of this test, he actually labels all the balls in the bag with the number "6." In the second iteration, with different subjects, he labels all the balls with the number "40." The result is that the first group value the wine at between "£6-£10", because they have just seen the number "6" on the ball, while the second group value the wine in the much higher range of "£20-60." Rational? Not at all! But Kahneman is demonstrating the power of suggestion that impacts our "impulsive" system.

Perhaps Dawkins would be right, that we should only act on complete information and evidence, if we were actually 100% rational beings. But in reality we are only 5% rational beings and 95% impulsive driven beings.

That is why rituals are so important. If we didn't train our "impulsive" (fast thinking) mind well as children, and later, as adults, then we would end up doing the wrong thing, even when we knew it was wrong.

A great example of this is another study that investigated[1] the non-return of library books across many libraries around the world. The analysis was done by book category and the fascinating observation was that the "ethics" category had a 50% higher non-return rate than non-ethics books! From which the researcher concluded that the intellectual understanding of morality has very little (or even, no) bearing on one's actual moral behavior.

Enter rituals. Rituals customize us to certain ingrained behaviors that TUNE our faster, more impulsive, decision-making system, and

---

1. Eric Schwitzgebel, "Do Ethicists Steal More Books?" *Philosophical Psychology*, 22 (2009), 711-725

increase the likelihood that our instinctive decision will be the right decision.

Rituals speak to our soul, a deeper level of our consciousness than our mind. The soul is the guide to our subconscious and hence rituals play a critical role in our decision-making process.

Chapter 39

JEWISH RITUALS HAVE DEEP MEANINGS

Rituals play a large part in Judaism. And each ritual has a message that has to be experienced before it can be understood.

The category of mitzvot, **Rituals**, includes:

i) Shabbat and festivals – with all their associated customs and practices

ii) *Tefillin* (prayer boxes), *tzitzit* (strings tied to the corner of a garment), and *kippah* (head covering) – ritual clothing for men

iii) Ritual food offerings and the Sabbatical year

Let's examine these rituals and the strong messages that they communicate.

Chapter 40

EVERY JEWISH FESTIVAL TEACHES US A LESSON

The Jewish calendar consists of the weekly Shabbat, regular festivals, and fast days throughout the year.

Each of these festive or solemn times bears a special message for Jews. And each message is critical for the Jewish people to fulfill their task in the world. In the next few chapters we will look at some of the key messages communicated by these rituals.

Festival	Primary Laws and Customs
Shabbat	i) Rest from many categories of creative work ii) Three special meals & wearing special clothes iii) Extra prayers and Torah readings throughout the day
Rosh Chodesh New Month	Festive service
Rosh Hashanah New Year	Blowing the shofar
Yom Kippur Day of Atonement	i) Fasting ii) Five prayer services iii) Wearing white (gowns for men, dresses for women)

Festival	Primary Laws and Customs
Succot Festival of Happiness	Eating (and sleeping) in a *Succah* for a whole week Shaking the *Lulav* and *Etrog* (the Four Species)
Simchat Torah Rejoicing with the Torah	Finishing the reading of the Torah and starting it again at the beginning.
Chanukah	Lighting the *Chanukiah* each night
Purim	i) Reading the Book of Esther ii) Giving food gifts to friends iii) Giving extra money to the poor iv) Eating a large celebratory meal
Pesach Festival of Freedom	i) Eating *Matzah*, not bread, for a whole week ii) Reading the *Hagaddah* (Exodus story) iii) Eating bitter herbs on the first night iv) Other special foods on the first night include – *carpas* (a vegetable aperitif), boiled egg in salt water, and *charoset* (a sweet nut paste).
Yom HaAtzmaut Israel's Day of Independence	Festivities Special services
Yom Yerushalayim Repatriation of Jerusalem	Festivities Special services
Shavuot Day of Giving the Torah	Festive service, custom to eat dairy food on first night Staying up to study the Torah all night long
Tisha B'Av	Fast day commemorating the destruction of the Temples

Chapter 41

SHABBAT – A TASTE OF THE WORLD TO COME

Say our Rabbis,

Shabbat is a taste of the world to come[1].

If a Jew is to dedicate his or her life to making peace on earth, then having a glimpse of what that peace might look like (or feel like) is a critical component.

And Shabbat does just that.

Shabbat laws consist of a number of "don'ts" and a number of "dos" and each of these contributes to a feeling of inner (or outer) peace.

The laws prohibiting creative work (*melachah*) force us to prepare for Shabbat before it comes in.

Our Rabbis say,

Only one who prepares on Friday, eats on Shabbat
(*Babylonian Talmud Avodah Zara 3a*)

While this makes Friday doubly tiring, it ensures that Shabbat itself is a day of rest. The double effort of Friday is represented symbolically at the Shabbat table by two challah loaves.[2]

Among other prohibitions, one is forbidden to cook on Shabbat, to

---

1. Babylonian Talmud Brachot 57b
2. The two loaves also remind us of the double portion of manna, collected in the desert, on Friday for Shabbat. (*Shemot*, Chapter 16)

drive, to use a computer or phone, to switch on (or off) the lights, or to plant, harvest, build, or write.

Strangely, many types of hard labor are permitted on Shabbat. For example, if I wanted to move a heavy bed, cupboard or table – that would be permitted. If I wanted to walk five miles across town to my grandparents home for a visit, that too would be permitted. And if I wanted to serve dinner to 100 guests and clear up afterwards, that too would be permitted.

So what is specifically forbidden on Shabbat?

It's not "work." It's "creative" work.

When God made the world, He chose not to complete it. Instead, He left a large proportion of the work for us to complete.

As it says in the second chapter of *Bereishit*:

"[On Shabbat] God rested from all the work that He created TO DO.*"*

What does it mean "work that He created to do?" It means that God didn't just create "things" during the first six days, but He also created "work" that had to BE DONE by mankind. On the seventh day God rested, not just from "creating things" but also from "creating more work."

So, too, the Torah commands us to refrain from "creative work" and from "kicking off more work."

For example:

Cooking is an act that changes the format of food (from raw to cooked) – so it's forbidden.

Planting a seed is an act that kicks off the process of growth – so that is forbidden.

Harvesting is an act that creates an edible product from a growing plant, so that's forbidden too.

Writing is an act that creates a document so that's forbidden.

Switching on electrical items – such as TVs, lights or phones – creates a new (electrical) connection that changes the color of the room, or enables us to communicate, work, or play. This is forbidden on Shabbat.

Building is a process that creates something useful (e.g., a house) out of things that are less useful (e.g., individual bricks) – so that too is forbidden.

And what's the psychological impact of Shabbat?

Well, there are at least two major impacts on our psyche from keeping Shabbat:

i) An appreciation of how much of our lives is actually spent "creating." In one way or another, we humans are machines for transforming reality from one state to another.

   a. Whether that's through business – agreeing, writing and signing contracts

   b. Or through writing – books, emails, texts

   c. Or cooking – converting raw ingredients into tasty concoctions

   d. Or through electronics – converting random electronic signals into meaningful communications through the use of a keypad.

ii) Shabbat is also an opportunity to recharge oneself from the stresses of the week past and prepare oneself for the excitement of the week ahead.

   a. Without a break we can't keep going

   b. Even a computer needs to be rebooted every so often or it, too, will eventually hang up with too much of its memory in use.

Shabbat, a regular break in one's life, is essential for the creative juices to keep running and for the enthusiasm for one's life mission to be recharged.

But there's an additional aspect to Shabbat, above and beyond just refraining from certain modes of work, and that's to "enjoy" Shabbat.

Clearly, enjoyment is mostly subjective, but the Torah outlines some essentials that provoke enjoyment for the majority. Key to these are eating three meals (two of which should have wine and meat), and wearing (better quality) clothes that are set aside just for Shabbat use.

Shabbat becomes a celebration, and not just a rest. We are commanded to spend more on Shabbat meals than we do during the week. And more on Shabbat clothes than we do on our weekday clothes.

These positive commandments (as opposed to the prohibitions above) emphasize the special nature of Shabbat – enabling us to celebrate the joy of recognizing God's creation. This is further enhanced by a longer synagogue service on a Shabbat morning where the Torah is read along with prayers that celebrate life, creation, and God's impact on our lives.

Our greatest day of enjoyment and rest is inextricably linked to God and His compassionate creation of the Universe, and so our feelings on Shabbat can generate an extraordinary passion for God.

Chapter 42

ROSH CHODESH –
A TIME OF OPTIMISM

Rosh Chodesh is the first day (or first two days) of the Jewish month.

The Jewish calendar is based on lunar months (28.5 days) rather than being a 12th of a solar year (29.5 days). The Jewish month begins when the moon reappears after it has been completely invisible. The middle of the month is therefore the full moon.

The spiritual message of Rosh Chodesh, celebrating with a special synagogue service and Torah reading, is one of optimism.

When the moon is at its smallest, pretty much invisible, *that's* when we celebrate the arrival of the New Month.

When things are at their darkest, *that's* when they're about to pick up.

When the Jewish people have had their darkest moments, *that's* when things began to get so much better.

The persecutions of the Middle Ages were followed by the Jewish renaissance in Israel and Poland. The persecutions in Poland and Russia in the 19th century were followed by the resurgence of Judaism through the Jews that emigrated to America in their millions. And the Holocaust was followed by the rebirth of the modern State of Israel.

Rosh Chodesh teaches us never to give up and that, after the darkest moments, we will see the greatest light. A people charged with making world peace must be able to continue through the toughest times with a positive attitude.

Chapter 43

ROSH HASHANAH–
REMEMBERING OUR MISSION

Rosh Hashanah, the New Year, is the time when we focus on the Mission statement of the Jewish people.

We blow the shofar, the ram's horn, to remind us of the world's pain. Three notes are blown in a regular pattern. One straight note followed by one or two broken notes, followed again by a straight note. Each of the straight notes must last at least as long as the total length of the broken notes, sounded between them. The sound of the shofar represents our lives.

Straight note #1:

Things are ticking along as usual

Broken note (or two) in the middle:

Something happens, unexpectedly, that shakes us up. Either externally or caused by our own incompetence or stupidity. We feel shaken, disturbed, uncertain. We can't see how things can ever be the same again.

Straight note #2:

Somehow we return to "normalcy," sometimes a slightly different normalcy, but our stress goes away in the end.

I attended a Stress Management course some years ago. The instructor explained how we grow through stress. She drew a picture of a circle and described it as our "zone of comfort."

Then she drew a larger circle around the first circle and explained that that was us working outside of our zone of comfort. The area between the two circles she shaded and labelled as "stress."

As we push ourselves into new areas of life, and new experiences, we suffer "stress" – the feeling that we can't cope. But, gradually, that energy is converted into "expansion" energy of the inner circle which slowly expands to fill the outer circle. The "zone of comfort" expands and the stress disappears as we grow through our experiences.

This is the message of the shofar:

The first straight blow represents our zone of comfort.

The second, broken, blow represents a shock to our system – a stress.

And the final blow represents our adapting to the new reality.

The shofar represents our process of continual improvement – moving towards our goals through expansion and consolidation.

And, as this is true for individuals, so it is true for society as a whole. Society is undergoing a process of continual improvement, often experienced as "shocks" such as war, disasters, and tragedies, from which we learn and improve to prevent the next disaster from occurring.

So on Rosh Hashanah we pray for divine help in overcoming our setbacks to achieve our purpose in the world. But what is that purpose?

One of the key prayers of the day[1] describes our vision of mankind coming together as "one organization."[2] Not as one faith, not as one ideology, but as "one organization." An organization has multiple divisions, departments, work groups and methodologies, but the thing that unites it is a common purpose. So, too, Jews pray on Rosh Hashanah that the all the nations of the world will find their

---

1. "Uv'chen ten pachdechah" which translates to "Instill your awe upon all Your works."
2. "Agudah Achat."

common purpose. Peace in the world will come when the nations of the world find their common purpose – and this will be achieved through the global adoption of the Noahide laws.

The message of the shofar and our prayers on Rosh Hashanah is, therefore, that the Jewish people should overcome all obstacles to bring the world to a state of peace.

This message is further reinforced by the three significant additions to the daily *Amidah* prayer – sections that describe God's Kingship, Remembrance, and the Shofar.

The Kingship section outlines the vision of Judaism – crowning God as King in the world, through the spreading of a global understanding of Monotheism (see Chapter 19). The Remembrance section connects us to our past – especially our forefathers Abraham, Isaac and Jacob – who dedicated their lives to achieving this aim of Kingship. And the Shofar section connects us to the sound of the shofar that is heard throughout the service and its eternal message of continual improvement and movement towards the vision of Kingship.

When we talk about crowning God as King, it may sound a little patronizing, after all, who are we to appoint God?! But, in truth, crowning God as King is more about us than it is about God.

Rabbi Adin Steinsaltz asks,[3] "Why is the lion called the king of the beasts? Surely man is stronger than a lion, after all how many men do you see in lion zoos?" And he answers – "Man can never be king of the beasts because man is not a beast!" In order to be the king, you have to be of the same species. So when we talk about crowning God as King, it means that we, mankind, must become more God-like in our behavior. Only once mankind is truly emulating God, will God be King over all of mankind.

---

3. "On the road with Rabbi Steinsaltz," Arthur Kurzweil, Jossey-Bass, 2006.

Chapter 44

YOM KIPPUR –
CONTINUAL IMPROVEMENT

Yom Kippur is the Holiest day of the Jewish calendar.

It's so holy that we refrain from the mundane activities of eating, drinking, washing ourselves, marital relations, and the comfort of leather shoes.

It was the day that the Holiest man, the High Priest, entered the Holiest location, the Holy of Holies in the depth of the Temple precinct.

Clearly Yom Kippur is tied up with the issue of "holiness."

But what is "holiness?"

When I ask this question, I am used to being told it is "sanctification." To which my usual response is "what, then, is sanctification?" Or, from budding Hebrew scholars, I am often given the answer "holiness is separation," but then I ask the question, "separation from what?!!"

Sadly, as Jews, we are accustomed to using terminology without (fully) understanding its meaning.

Rav Kook,[1] explains the meaning of "holiness." Based on a statement in the Talmud that "there is no reciting of the Holiness prayer with less than ten men (i.e., a *minyan*)," Rav Kook asks, "what is the connection between holiness and having a quorum of men in synagogue?" And he answers in the following vein.

> There are two ways to live our life. Most of us, most of the time, live our lives thinking mainly about ourselves – our interests, our needs and our desires. But occasionally each of us will make a decision, not

---

1.   In his commentary on the Siddur, *Olat Reiyah*.

for ourselves, but with the majority, the community, in mind. That is a moment of "holiness." And, hence, the "Holiness" prayer that is recited in the repetition of the Amidah each day requires ten men to be present, representing the community. When we recite the words "Holy, holy, holy" we can look at the crowd around us and immediately understand that "holiness" is thinking about the greater good – about the community that is represented by the quorum of ten.

The "holiness" of Yom Kippur is therefore connected to a way of life that is directed at the whole, not the individual. The act of the High Priest, who risks his life by entering the Holy of Holies and performing a ritual, on behalf of the community, that must be done with complete accuracy or his life could be forfeit – is an act of pure altruism.

Only a people who put God firmly in the middle of their circle can truly ascribe equal importance to others as to themselves. So Yom Kippur is about putting God in the middle of our circles and realizing that we are equidistant to God with the rest of humanity.

But, just as the shofar on Rosh Hashanah reminds us to persevere through all obstacles, Yom Kippur is also a sort of "Reset" button for the Jewish mission.

The difference is that Yom Kippur encourages us to overcome our internal obstacles to change.

Our passion for our mission may have waned over the previous year, so Yom Kippur is the day that God wipes the slate clean and allows us to try harder in the year to come. The very timing of Yom Kippur, ten days after Rosh Hashanah, the New Year, testifies to this "new start."

How so?

Rosh Hashanah is the beginning of the new year.

Yom Kippur is the day that we assess our successes and failures for the year past.

Normally one would expect one year to end and then the new one to begin. But in Judaism, the new year begins BEFORE the previous one has ended! And as this is true for the year, so this is true for all units of Jewish time.

Consider this. The Jewish day begins at sunset, but the previous day doesn't end until nightfall (roughly an hour later). The new Jewish month, six times a year, is two days long[2] – we bring it in a day before the previous month has ended. The Jewish week ends with Shabbat, but Shabbat also represents the beginning of the week ahead. The seventh year of the Sabbatical cycle ends six years of fruitful agri-culture, but it also marks the beginning of the next cycle.

Jewish time, exemplified by Rosh Hashanah and Yom Kippur, days, weeks, months, years, and Sabbaticals, is not linear but overlapping. Each time period begins before the previous one has ended.

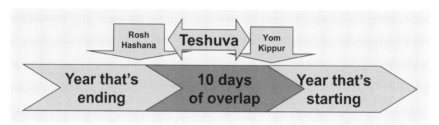

This gives us the opportunity to do "Teshuvah" – to "improve" in the interim period – once we've moved on to the next time slot, but before we have to stand up and account for our inadequacies of the previous time slot. It's optimal timing for those who struggle to hit deadlines.

The ten days between Rosh Hashanah and Yom Kippur are called the Days of Repentance and these days are spent in introspection and committing ourselves to do better in the year ahead.

Overlapping time is "continual improvement" time. The first thing we have to undergo in each new year is an introspection of our lives in the year just past. And that can be the launch pad for doing a better job in the year ahead. And human psychology is such that sometimes we have to have the shock of a new year starting before we actually get round to making amends for the year just past.

---

2.   The other six months have only one day Rosh Chodesh

Chapter 45

SUCCOT –
HAPPY WITH THE BASICS

Succot is a festival of "happiness" which is surprising, considering that the main commandment of Succot is to live in a leaky hut for a whole week!

Reasonably one might ask the question, "Why am I living in a simple hut for a week when I'm meant to be happy?!"

And, simply, the answer is – Succot is a festival of appreciation and satisfaction. On Succot we build simple temporary structures (for a few dollars) with a leaky roof – and we live in them. Every Jew, in every country in the world, is commanded to do this.

Some Jews may leave their million dollar mansions to sit in the Succah. Others may sit in a Succah built in the parking space of their council apartment block. Succot is an equalizer. On Succot there's no "them" and "us." There's only "us."

A Succah can be built, and enjoyed, for under $100. It's not as comfortable as our regular home, but it works. And it reminds us of something that we so often forget with all the distractions of work and competing with our neighbors. It reminds us that, so often, the simple things in life are the most important. On Succot it's not the building that matters, but the company that matters. We sit in the Succah with friends, family, and guests and eat, drink, and sing. Money can't buy the pleasure that can be derived from this simple living. But even so, one wouldn't want to spend more than a week in the Succah. The Succah is a demonstration of the power of a mitzvah to turn a basic physical event into a far more pleasurable spiritual experience.

There's a beautiful (perhaps allegorical) story told about Yitzchak Perlman – the famous violinist.

Childhood polio left Perlman able to walk only with braces on both legs and crutches. When Perlman plays at a concert, the journey from the wings to the center of the stage is long and slow. Yet, when he plays, his talent transcends any thought of physical challenge.

On November 18th, 1995, at the Lincoln Center in New York, Perlman was scheduled to play a difficult, challenging violin concerto. In the middle of the performance one of the strings on his violin snapped with a rifle-like popping noise that filled the entire auditorium. The orchestra immediately stopped playing and the audience held its collective breath. The assumption was that he would have to put on his braces, pick up his crutches, and leave the stage.

Either that or someone would have to come out with another string or replace the violin. After a brief pause, Perlman set his violin under his chin and signaled to the conductor to begin.

One person in the audience reported what happened: "I know it is impossible to play a violin concerto with only three strings. I know that and so do you, but that night, Yitzchak Perlman refused to know it.

You could see him modulating, changing, and recomposing in his head. At one point it sounded as if he were re-tuning the strings to get a new sound that had never been heard before."

When he finished, there was an awesome silence that filled the room. Then people rose and cheered. Perlman smiled, wiped his brow, and raised the bow of his violin to quiet them. He spoke, not boastfully, but quietly in a pensive tone,

"You know, sometimes it is the artist's task to find out how much music you can still make with what you have left."

The audience exploded in applause, smiling ecstatically at what they had all witnessed.[1]

We are emotionally attuned to the creation of something from nothing – such as the formation of beautiful music from a simple wooden instrument. Our souls sing with the greatness than comes from simplicity.

---

1. As reported in the Houston Chronicle, February 10, 2001.

The Succah breeds an appreciation for simplicity and camaraderie, across all social barriers of mankind, an independence from materialism. It's the sort of joy that people get from camping with a group of friends, but it's done in one's own garden, and sleeping in the Succah is not compulsory if it gets too cold!

Nevertheless, for a people charged with spreading the concept of One God, in the middle of the circle, Who spreads the "tabernacle of His peace over all of us" – the feeling of solidarity that one gets from a Succah speaks far more than words.

And it is the concept of solidarity that is reinforced by the other major ritual on Succot – the "Four Species." We bind together a palm branch, two willow branches, and three myrtle branches and shake them together with a citron (an "etrog").

The Rabbis explain that these elements symbolize four different types of human beings. If, symbolically, flavor represents good deeds (i.e. keeping the commandments) and smell represents Torah knowledge, then:

i) the etrog (which has both flavor and taste) represents those Jews who have both learning and good deeds

ii) the palm branch (which is odorless but bares tasty dates) represents those who have good deeds but no knowledge

iii) the myrtle (which has a beautiful smell but no fruit) represents those who have knowledge but no deeds

iv) and the willow (which has neither smell nor taste) represents those who have neither learning nor good deeds.

By shaking them all together, we symbolize the need for all types of Jew in the world. If peace is about bringing people together in a framework of understanding, without necessarily trying to change others to be more like ourselves, then the Four Species are a beautiful symbol of that peace.

In this picture of the Four Species, the willow seems to be the loser – without Torah learning nor good deeds (i.e., mitzvot). And, yet, there's a fascinating story that I heard from a Professor of Pharmaceutical History[2] that tells us otherwise . . .

---

2. Dr. Walter Sneader, based on a speech that he delivered at the Royal Society of

The most important medicine in the history of the world – with over 100 billion units sold – is the Aspirin. A pain killer par excellence – it was discovered by people who lived down river from willow trees that overhang into the water.

The water that they drank was claimed to have miraculous pain killing powers. And a German company, Bayer, was the first to synthesize salicylic acid – found naturally in willow bark.

A German chemist, named Felix Hoffmann, is credited with the development of aspirin while working at the German company Bayer's pharmaceutical laboratory.

However, regarding the true inventor of aspirin, there is a contradictory claim, which has mostly been ignored. The claim was made by Alfred Eichengrün, a German Jewish chemist, in a paper he wrote in 1949.

Eichengrün, who had been Hoffmann's boss at Bayer's pharmaceutical lab, claimed that he had instructed Hoffmann to synthesize acetylsalicylic acid. So HE was responsible for the discovery of aspirin.

Indeed, Eichengrün explained, Hoffmann had not even known why he was performing the task, which he only undertook under instruction from his supervisor.

So who was this Alfred Eichengrün? And why might his claim be credible?

Eichengrün was a prolific inventor of chemical compounds who held 47 patents. He joined Bayer relatively early in his career and quickly ascended the ranks of the company.

Eichengrün made some notable achievements in his time at Bayer. He'd discovered the treatment for gonorrhoea. And during the 1st World War he developed a type of plastic named Cellon, which was used for gas masks and pilots' goggles in the First World War, and a cellulose acetate that rendered aeroplane wings water resistant.

Eichengrün had opened his own manufacturing plant, which he called Cellon-Werke. There he pioneered the process of injection molding of plastics so effectively that his practices are still used today.

Chemistry's Annual Conference in Edinburgh in 1999.

"Hoffmann didn't understand why he was doing the work," Dr. Sneader, the notable pharmaceutical historian, stated. "He was just a technician."

The discovery of aspirin occurred in 1934, a year after the Nazis came to power and Eichengrun was keeping a low profile. In fact, in 1944, he was sent to Theresienstadt at the age of 76.

While he languished in the camp, Eichengrün sent a letter to Bayer asking for help. He pointed to his years of service to the company and the highly valuable contributions he had a made, which included the invention of aspirin.

Bayer ignored the letter, which is today in the company's archives.

So Eichengrün remained at Theresienstadt until Soviet troops liberated the camp in May 1945, when he was 78 years old.

Eichengrun is the archetypal Jewish Willow – he was not a "religious" Jew, he had neither exceptional Jewish learning, nor was he observant. But his contribution to improving the world – providing people in the poorest countries with affordable pain-killing drugs – is no less impressive than the contributions of many of our most learned and religiously observant brethren.

Jews like Eichengrun make us proud to shake all four species together.

And remind us to recognize and respect others for their unique contributions and skills.

Chapter 46

SIMCHAT TORAH – OUR LEARNING NEVER ENDS

Simchat Torah, which comes at the end of the festival of Succot, is the day that we complete the annual reading of the Torah by reading from the end of the book of *Devarim* and when we commence the reading of the Torah again, from the beginning of the book of *Bereishit*.

The fact that we read a portion of the Torah every Shabbat morning is already an indication of the importance of learning in Judaism. But nothing compares to the level of joy and celebration that we experience on Simchat Torah (literally "rejoicing with the Torah"). And this joy transmits a strong message to us and to our children that there is nothing more satisfying in life than studying Torah.

Often with our studies it is not until we get to the more complex aspects that we can truly appreciate the depth of wisdom in what we are learning. But we have to work hard to get there. And while we are repetitively learning the "ABCs" or the "simplification of fractions," we can often get a little despondent with our subject and, even, occasionally give up completely.

That's the genius of Simchat Torah – we get to feel the joy of having reached the zenith of our learning, for a short time, even though we have not actually reached it. And that feeling is held inside us and can motivate us to work a little harder on our studies in the year ahead – just so we might feel it again.

Simchat Torah is a festival that reminds us of the importance of learning. And learning is an essential precondition for changing ourselves and the world.

Chapter 47

CHANUKAH – SPREADING THE LIGHT

Chanukah is a festival that speaks to the heart of the Jewish project.

Some two-and-a-half thousand years ago, the mighty Greek army invaded the Temple in Jerusalem, desecrating it and putting it out of operation. At the same time, a band of Jewish warriors, the Maccabees, arose and fought the Greeks, recaptured the Temple, and rededicated it to God.

What is most fascinating about the eight day festival of Chanukah is that it is not the military battle that is our key focus. Rather it is the "spiritual" victory of regaining the Temple and lighting the Menorah with a day's worth of oil that miraculously lasted eight days.

Today, Jews celebrate Chanukah with a *Chanukiah*, a nine branch candelabra that looks remarkably like the Menorah, but with two more branches. The central light[1] is lit each night as a sort of "pilot light." And then each night, the same number of lights as the night itself is lit. That leads to two lights on the first night, three on the second, up to nine on the final night.

Rav Kook[2] explained the significance of this increasing light. In his words, the role of the Jewish people is to increase light in the world – that light being the understanding of God. Despite the foundation of this festival being our persecution at the hands of idolaters (i.e., the ancient Greeks), the message is one of "spreading the love" – a message of tolerance and coexistence – bringing God into the middle of our circle – the message of Monotheism.

---

1. Technically this light does not have to be central, but distinguished from the other lights by being at a different height from them.
2. In his commentary on the aggadot of Gemara Shabbat, *Ein Ayah*.

Chapter 48

PURIM – SELFLESSNESS PAYS

Purim is a festival that has predominantly four commandments:

i) The reading of the Book of Esther

ii) Delivering a food package[1] to at least one friend

iii) Giving charity to at least two poor people

iv) Celebrating with a festive meal

What these commandments have in common is "selflessness."

The story of Esther is the story of a Jewish woman who was selected to be Queen of Persia by beauty parade, against her wishes. Once Queen, she and her uncle discovered a plot by the Prime Minister to exterminate the whole Jewish people. In order to stop this extermination, she had to petition the King, doubly risking her life – firstly, by revealing her own identity as a Jewess and, secondly, by entering his court un-summoned, an act punishable by death. Yet she did so and succeeded in having the decree overturned, the Jewish people saved, and the Jews were even given the right to exterminate their enemies.

Esther models the ideal of "selflessness."

And then there's the commandment of giving to the poor. Charity is a constant commandment in Judaism, but on Purim there is an extra requirement to give substantially to two individuals – again thinking of others.

---

1. The food package must contain at least two types of food that require different blessings – such as bread and wine, or cake and fruit.

The sending of a food parcel to a friend is yet another way of considering others on our day of celebration, creating a feeling of a shared communal experience.

And the festive meal is further opportunity to bring others to our tables and include them in our celebrations.

On Purim, there is a focus on selflessness. But, unlike Chanukah, there is also a focus on destroying evil – specifically in self defense. What connects these two concepts of destroying evil and acting selflessly?

The message of Purim is that the Jewish people have encountered, will encounter, and continue to encounter, evil regimes that protest against tolerance and equality in the world. Sometimes these regimes have to be destroyed. But fighting is never justified out of pure self-interest, it is only justified as a form of self-defense and "for the greater good."

For this reason, celebrating the downfall of our enemies must be undertaken cautiously, with a strong focus on selflessness, otherwise human nature can justify atrocities against others just for being different – and a major task of the Jewish people is to fight *against* intolerance.

Indeed, in our daily prayers we recite the *Amidah* (also known as "the Eighteen Blessings") three times a day. Strangely, the *Amidah* prayer contains nineteen prayers, not eighteen. Some 1,500 years ago an additional prayer was composed by an obscure Rabbi, Shmuel HaKatan, a prayer against the enemies of the Jewish people. Importantly, the only other reference to Shmuel HaKatan in Jewish literature is his advice in the Talmud "not to rejoice in the downfall of our enemies." Says Rav Kook[2] only someone who held no schadenfreude, bad wishes towards others, could rightfully compose a prayer calling for the downfall of our enemies. The destruction of others is not something to celebrate but, rather, an occasional requirement for self preservation.

---

2. Rav Kook, Commentary on the aggadot of the Talmud Brachot, *Ein Ayah*. See also the beautiful commentary of Rabbi Lord Jonathan Sacks, *Hebrew Daily Prayer Book*, Collins, 2006.

Chapter 49

PESACH – VALUING OUR FREEDOM

Pesach, Passover, is the festival that celebrates the Jews leaving slavery in Egypt over 3,000 years ago.

The festival is celebrated for a whole week and special foods are prepared that contain no leavened components (such as bread, cake, yeast, and pasta) and, for many Jews, no rice or pulses. The festival kicks off with a large dinner where the Haggadah, a historical account with blessings and psalms, is read and special foods are consumed.

But everything is structured to open our hearts to the value of FREEDOM.

The foods include:

i) *Matzah* – unleavened bread

ii) *Maror* – bitter herbs (usually fresh grated horseradish)

iii) *Charoset* – a sweet fruity, nutty paste

iv) *Carpas* – a small portion of vegetable, such as parsley or potato, dipped into salt water

v) Boiled eggs dipped into salt water

The majority of the symbols have a single message, reminding us of the pain of slavery or the joy of freedom.

For example:

Maror, the bitter herbs, are there to remind us of the pain of slavery.

Boiled eggs in salt water remind us of the tears we cried in Egypt.

Carpas, the vegetable aperitif, on the other hand, reminds us of the joy of being free – it is eaten before the meal as an appetizer, which was a standard course for freemen in the time of the Roman Empire.

Additionally, it is customary to lean to the right while we eat the special foods, just as free Romans would have leaned on couches during their meals. And it is customary for us to pour the four cups of wine for others, and let them pour for us, representing another aspect of freedom – waiter(ess) service!

Most remarkable, however, are the *matzah* and *charoset*.

The *charoset*, a sweet paste symbolizing the cement that we had to mix as slaves in Egypt, is a symbol of slavery, but it is sweet and delicious. The symbolism here suggests that there is almost something enticing about being a slave. Certainly there is a lack of responsibility and it is well known that prisoners, on being released, as well as boarding school children and soldiers on coming home, can suffer a "debunking syndrome." *Charoset* reminds us that slavery is evil, even if we can find pleasurable aspects within it.

And *matzah*, too, has a dual message. On the one hand it reminds us of the bread we ate as slaves – when we would not have had time to bake real bread. On the other hand, it reminds us of the bread we ate on escaping, when we left in a hurry and had no time to let it rise, until we crossed the Red Sea and were truly free. So Matzah is both the bread of slavery and the bread of freedom. Matzah reminds us that there may not be a huge material benefit in being free – our standard of living may even fall in a free society. However, the spiritual value of freedom is so great that it is even worth suffering to become free.

Pesach teaches us that Freedom is a value that we should treasure and appreciate – both for ourselves and for others. And so it is not surprising that inspiration from the Pesach story has led to the liberation of slaves, all over the world, during the past millennia.

Quoting from Martin Luther King's famous speech:[1]

> *"The Bible tells the thrilling story of how Moses stood in Pharaoh's court centuries ago and cried, "Let my people go." This is a kind of open-*

---

1. Nobel Lecture, December, 1964

ing chapter in a continuing story. The present struggle in the United States is a later chapter of the same unfolding story."

A critical part of the Monotheistic message is "God is in the middle." Not you, not me, but God. That makes all of us equal, in the eyes of our Creator, and doesn't leave any room for the enslavement of others.

Chapter 50

YOM HA'ATZMAUT – COMING HOME

Since the destruction of the Second Temple, some 2,000 years ago, Jews have been dispersed around the world, away from their homeland, Israel.

Following the atrocities of the Holocaust, the Nations of the world formed an organization, the United Nations, with its Charter of Human Rights, in order to prevent such an atrocity happening again.[1]

One of the first votes for the nascent United Nations was for the establishment of a Jewish homeland in Israel. The vote took place in 1947. It was carried by a narrow majority and led to the Declaration of Independence of the State of Israel on the 5th day of the Jewish month of Iyar, in 1948.

The Jewish prophets refer, over and over again, to the return of the Jews to Israel, as a precursor to the Messianic Age where peace will prevail between nations.

Apparently, God wished that the Jewish people would be dispersed across the world for two millennia in order to spread the message of Monotheism to the Nations. But now the time has come for us to return home.

Yom Ha'Atzmaut celebrates our return to Israel to fulfill the next part of our destiny as a people. This we will discuss further in the final chapters of the book.

---

1. Stated by Ban Ki Moon, Secretary General of the UN, on 27/1/14 reported by UN News Centre.

Chapter 51

YOM YERUSHALAYIM – RETURNING TO ZION

But, in 1948, our return to our land was incomplete. Half of Jerusalem remained in the hands of Jordan, and the Temple Mount, the holiest location in the world, was not under Jewish control, nor was it even accessible to Jews.

In 1967 this changed within a week. Five Arab nations waged war simultaneously with the young Jewish State – Egypt, Syria, Lebanon, Jordan, and Iraq. The whole world was on tenterhooks, expecting another Holocaust, after all, how could the small Jewish army defend itself against forces ten times as large?

And yet, a miracle occurred. Within six days not only had the Jewish State succeeded in defending itself, but it had also recaptured Jerusalem (along with the West Bank, Golan Heights, and half of Egypt)!

This was the completion of the Zionist dream – literally the return to Zion, the Temple Mount. But things were not so straightforward.

In the words of my teacher, Rabbi Menachem Schrader, "Before the Six Day War no Jew could have imagined that, in possession of the Temple Mount, we would not immediately rebuild the Temple. However, immediately after the Six Day War, no Jew could imagine that, now, in possession of the Temple Mount, we would ever rebuild the Temple."

So, what happened in just six days to change the aspirations of a whole people? The answer is in our prayer book.

Toward the end of our *Amidah* prayer, recited three times daily, we have three requests that don't seem to fit into a logical order:

i) The prayer for the rebuilding of Jerusalem

ii) The prayer for our "voices to be heard"

iii) The prayer for the rebuilding of the Temple ("*Retzei*")

Up till this point in the *Amidah*, the order of the prayers is pretty clear. We pray, chronologically, for the ingathering of the exiles, the reestablishment of Jewish leadership in Israel, the rebuilding of Jewish learning institutions, and the defeat of our enemies. So the request for Jerusalem and the Temple are perfectly logical in their order.

Why, however, is there a prayer for our voices to be heard in the middle?

And here we can ask the question, "Who needs to hear our voices?" If it is God, then, as we have said before, He doesn't need anything, even our prayers. Apparently, the ones who must hear our voices are: us!

We have prayed for the rebuilding of the Temple during thousands of years of painful exile and we continue to pray for the rebuilding of the Temple on a daily basis. Our voices can be heard pouring out every Tisha B'Av in anguish, crying out for the return to our holiest mountain.

And yet, somewhere between the prayers for Jerusalem and the prayers for the Temple, there's a blockage. And that blockage is: us.

If the Jewish people wished to rebuild the Temple, it is now in the middle of the modern Jewish State, it is more feasible than ever. When will we listen to our own voices?

The prayer, *Shema Koleinu*, "hear our voices," is directed at *us*. When we collectively take the time to listen to our own requests for the rebuilding of the Temple, that's when it will happen. But not before.

Yom Yerushalayim is a celebration of the return of the Temple Mount to Jewish sovereignty, but it is also a reminder that we Jews have to continue to work on our own resolve if we are to progress the vision of world peace.

Chapter 52

SHAVUOT – RECEIVING OUR INSTRUCTION SET

Shavuot is the festival that commemorates the giving of the Torah to the Jewish people at Mount Sinai.

Between Pesach and Shavuot there are seven weeks (forty-nine days) that we count each night, from one to forty-nine.

Shavuot (literally the Festival of "Weeks") is the only festival in the Torah that is not given a date. We are just told that it is seven weeks from Pesach.

So this has led some Rabbis to describe Shavuot as a sort of continuation[1] of Pesach. So what is the connection between Pesach – the festival of physical freedom – and Shavuot, the giving of the Torah?

One popular answer is that Pesach is the festival of "freedom from" (slavery). Shavuot is the festival of "freedom to" (fulfill the Torah).

Rav Adin Steinsaltz[2] describes this beautifully with an analogy. If you take a lion that was born in captivity, out of its cage at the zoo, you notice a strange phenomenon. It may wander around the zoo, terrorizing visitors for a while, but when it comes to dinner time, the lion will wander back into the cage. For the lion, dinner is served in the cage. It does not have sufficient imagination, once fully grown, to envision what food could be, if not thrown into the cage by its keeper. My children discovered this recently for themselves when their pet Siberian hamster, Cookie, escaped from his cage for a week. The children were terribly distraught for seven days, but, leaving the cage door open, with the food inside, Cookie eventually realized

---

1. For example, the Netivot Shalom. He describes the 49 days of the Omer as a sort of long Chol HaMoed.
2. "On the road with Rabbi Steinsaltz," Arthur Kurzweil, Jossey-Bass, 2006.

that life was easier for him (or her?) in captivity, and that's how we found him again, munching away on his bran flakes.

Well, that's us too. And that was the Jewish people coming out of Egypt. Left to their own devices, complaining about the lack of water and the repetitive food, the Jewish people would certainly have returned to captivity rather than wander the desert for forty years. They wouldn't have even been able to dream about the benefits of freedom, because they had no inkling of what they could do with that freedom.

But after forty-nine days of journeying they reached Mount Sinai and received the Torah. The Torah is the "blueprint" of Creation, the instruction manual for humankind. The Torah gave them a vision of a world where they were not slaves. Indeed, a world where there were no slaves at all.[3] Where men and women could be free to live in peace and to build societies where every person would be valued.

Shavuot is the celebration of receiving our life instruction manual – the Torah.

---

3. The Torah does refer to slaves – Jewish and non-Jewish slaves. However, if one looks at the small print, the laws of dealing with slaves are so restrictive that it effectively abolishes the institution of slavery as we would understand it today. For example, a master is not able to eat before feeding his slave, nor is he able to eat better food than his slave!

Chapter 53

TISHA B'AV – LEARNING FROM OUR MISTAKES

Tisha B'Av is the most important fast day in the Jewish calendar (after Yom Kippur). It commemorates the destruction of both Temples (which occurred over 500 years apart, but both in the same week of the year in the month of Av).

The story is told in the Babylonian Talmud about the beginning of the sequence of events that led to the destruction of the Second Temple by the Romans (in the 1st century CE).

> In the ancient city of Jerusalem lived a man named Kamza and another man named Bar Kamza. A third man, who was a friend of Kamza and an enemy of Bar Kamza, threw a wedding for his daughter and ordered his servant to invite Kamza. By mistake, Bar Kamza was invited. He turned up and sat at his table. When the man saw his enemy, Bar Kamza, he immediately went up to him and demanded that he leave the wedding. Bar Kamza pleaded, "Don't embarrass me – let me pay for my dinner and stay." But the man insisted. Bar Kamza made a further offer, "Let me pay for half your wedding . . . for the **whole** wedding, but don't embarrass me!" The man refused and threw him out the wedding. Bar Kamza noticed that there were some senior Rabbis there, and they didn't protest.

> So Bar Kamza, himself a Jew, said to himself, "If those Rabbis didn't protest, they must have agreed with me being thrown out. I will make trouble for the Jews." Bar Kamza went to the Romans and told them that the Jewish people were planning a rebellion against Rome. The Roman Emperor demanded that he prove this. So Bar Kamza said, "Send an animal offering to their Temple and you'll see that they will not offer it." The Romans sent Bar Kamza with a young bull as an offering. On the way to the Temple, Bar Kamza made a small wound

in its eyelid in such a place that would not render it an invalid offering by the Romans, but would by the Jews.

When the animal reached the Temple, the Rabbis argued, "It has a blemish. If we don't offer it, the Romans will kill us, unless we kill Bar Kamza so they don't find out. But then people might say that the punishment for offering a blemished bull is the death penalty. But if we do offer it, then people might say that it is OK to offer a blemished animal on the altar." In the end the Rabbis refused the offering and let Bar Kamza return to the Romans. Because of the indecision of the Rabbis, Jerusalem was destroyed.

The message of this story, and that of many other stories about disasters that have occurred to the Jewish people over the ages, is – we Jews brought the suffering upon OURSELVES!

We mourn the destruction of the Temple, but we also mourn the behavior of our people at the time of the destruction, which our Rabbis termed "Causeless Hatred." So Tisha B'Av, a day of fasting and mourning, is not just in remembrance of what we once had but, rather, an exercise in introspection, as a people, to ask, "How can we ensure this doesn't happen again?"

A people charged with moving the world forwards must have mechanisms to learn from their mistakes. Tisha B'Av is one of those mechanisms.

Chapter 54

MALE RITUALS –
TEFILLIN, TALLIT, AND KIPPAH

Another category of ritual in Judaism is ritual objects that are worn – especially for men. Again each item has a strong message that is meant to be conveyed through its usage.

TEFILLIN (PRAYER BOXES)

Tefillin consist of two small, black, leather boxes, one of which is strapped around the left arm[1] while the other is strapped above the forehead.

Men wear their *tefillin* during weekday morning services.

The boxes contain parchments with the four sections in the Torah that relate the commandment of wearing tefillin. Two of these are the first two sections of the *Shema* prayer.

In order to understand the meaning behind this commandment, let's ask some important questions about the *tefillin*.

i) Why are they strapped to the arm and to the forehead?

ii) Why is the word for head *tefillin* in the Torah, "*totafot,*" which the Rabbis identify as being one of the few foreign words in the Torah – seemingly emanating from the Ancient Egyptian?

iii) Why is God's name spelled out by the straps, as we wrap it around our hands and with the strap on our heads?

---

1. Actually the arm of the weaker hand (that we do not use to write with).

Fig 2.2 Depiction of the Ancient Egyptian goddess Isis   (Jeff Dahl, Wikipedia)

An interesting way to look at tefillin is to understand that the head *tefillin* – the *totafot* – was worn by the Ancient Egyptian goddess, Isis, in iconography.

The *totafot* was worn as a sort of crown and was in the shape of a throne – in fact the very name Isis means "throne." Isis was the goddess over all the kings – seemingly the supreme power in Egypt.

The head *tefillin* therefore seems to resemble a sort of crown, depicting status and power.

The key difference between the Jewish head *tefillin* and that of Isis is the contents. In the case of Isis, the crown was there to display her power and supremacy. In the case of the head *tefillin*, the contents remind us of our obligation to spread the concept of the One God. In our case, the power and supremacy on display are not our own, but God's.

This also explains the spelling out of God's name (SH-D-AY) on the hand and head with the straps – to remind us that *God* is being glorified in the wearing of the tefillin.

And why the arm *tefillin*? Well, if the head *tefillin* reminds us of God's supremacy and we wear it next to our brain – the site of thought –– then the arm *tefillin* lies close to our heart – the site of emotion. Its strap winds around our arm and hand – the site of action. Altogether the *tefillin* are there to focus our thoughts, feelings, and actions on the pursuit of God and Godliness through the prayers and through the commandments.

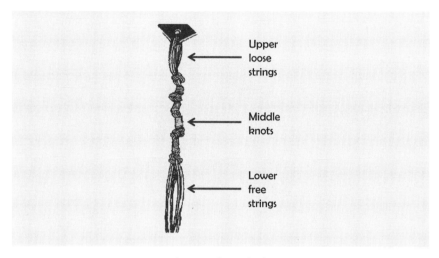

Fig 2.3 The Tzitzit

TZITZIT

There are two garments that a Jewish man is likely to wear that would have *tzitzit* attached – the *tzitzit katan* (a vest) and the *tallit* (a prayer shawl). Both of these are four cornered garments – the *tzitzit katan* are traditionally worn all day, whereas the *tallit* is worn only during morning services (and on Yom Kippur). The *tzitzit* themselves are tassels, and each is made from four strings tied together with knots and windings.

The *tzitzit* remind us of the commandments – because the Gematria (numerology) together with the number of knots and windings represent the number 613, the total number of commandments in the Torah.

But the main message of the *tzitzit* is described best by Rabbi Samson Rafael Hirsch.[2]

---

2.   *Collected Writings*, Feldheim.

The *tzitzit* have a top section which consists of loose strings above the knots. And a middle section consisting of tightly wound strings and knots. And a bottom section of free strings.

Says Rabbi Hirsch, the commandments can be looked at, cynically, as restricting our lives – "don't work on Shabbat, don't eat pig, don't eat on Yom Kippur!" – and that's the symbolism of the knots and windings – heavy restrictions. Above the knots is a loose section – that's how we imagine our life might be had we not been restricted by our commitments to the Torah.

However, below the knots, there is an even freer section of totally loose strings. And this, explains Rabbi Hirsch, shows the reality of the mitzvot. They don't tie us down. In actuality, they liberate us.

The *tzitzit* symbolize the fact that the truest form of freedom is having obligations. We see this in life when we take time off from work. Initially we feel liberated by a relaxing holiday on the beach. Eventually we start to get itchy feet and find something else to fill our time. Having complete freedom is a paradoxical form of slavery. We need boundaries in life to enable us to progress in a straight line.

We also understand this, intuitively, in the way that we bring up children. Children who are given no boundaries will find trouble and suffer in their studies, sports, and social development. By guiding our children through some sort of educational and behavioral framework (with the help of school and religion), we enable them to learn, play, and develop as human beings.

I remember returning to London, from Israel, after my rabbinical studies. That week I went shopping at the local supermarket with my five-year-old daughter, Maia, and four-year-old daughter, Keren. As we approached the check-out there were the usual array of tempting candies and Maia and Keren, naturally, each picked up a packet and beckoned to me, eagerly, to buy them. I looked at the packets and saw that they contained non-kosher ingredients and so I told them, "Sorry! They're not kosher!" To my surprise and satisfaction, instead of complaining and insisting, they put the packets back and that was the end of the conversation. I realized at that moment the true power of the mitzvot. Here were candies that were certainly delicious and tempting, and yet with two words, "not kosher," my young daughters knew that they couldn't have them. What an education for life! How many temptations are they likely to have in the future? Drugs, relationships, expensive items that they cannot afford. How important it is to be educated, early on, that not everything that is tempting is permissible.

And that is the message of tzitzit. The mitzvot are liberating because they help to define for us what is permissible and what is forbidden, and prevent us from wasting our time trying to achieve the unobtainable or the detrimental.

KIPPAH

The kippah (ritual head covering) is probably the most noticeable symbol of Judaism on the street. The symbolism of the kippah is simple. It helps us to remember that there is Something above us, and it identifies us as Jews. These are two ways to guide us away from temptations and sin: firstly, through keeping us focused on the presence of God and, secondly, by making us aware that others will formulate their views of Judaism through our behavior.

The Talmud[3] relates that a woman was once told by astrologers that her son was destined to be a thief. To prevent this from happening, she insisted that he always have his head covered, to remind him of G-d's presence and instil within him the fear of heaven. Once, while sitting under a palm tree, his head covering fell off. He was suddenly overcome by an urge to eat a fruit from the tree, which did not belong to him. It was then that he realized the strong effect which the wearing of a kippah had on him.

Today one can observe a variety of kippot and, in the Charedi community, black hats. All of these head coverings serve the same purpose to remind us of Who is watching us.

---

3.   Shabbat 156b, summarized by Baruch Davidson, Chabad.org.

Chapter 55

PRIESTS –
THE ULTIMATE BLESSING

Out of the 613 mitzvot in the Torah, at least 200 are involved with Temple activities, such as sacrifices, that we can't perform today in the absence of a Temple.

However, out of these hundreds of mitzvot there is a small handful that we *can* fulfill today, at the level of a rabbinical law, rather than a Torah law.

One of these laws is the Priestly Blessing.

During morning and additional services each day in Israel, but only on holidays outside of Israel, the male Cohanim (priestly caste) come to the front of the synagogue to bless the congregation. The Cohanim are the men in the community who have a tradition, going back millennia, that they are descended from Moses' brother Aaron, the High Priest, at the time of the Torah.

In the middle of the repetition of the *Amidah* prayer, they face the community and recite the blessing, "Blessed are you God . . . who commands us to bless the Jewish people with Love."

They then continue to recite the Priestly Blessing exactly as it appears in Bamidbar,

> *"May God bless you and keep you."*
> *"May God light up your face and be gracious to you."*
> *"May God lift up His face towards you and may He grant you peace."*

Why did the blessing have to be given by the Cohanim, the priests? And why did it have to be given with "love?"

And the answer is subtle.[1] The Germans have given us a term –
schadenfreude – getting satisfaction from the distress of others.
When we wish success for others, it is always limited. It is difficult
for any human being (except perhaps a parent) to wish someone
to be more successful than themselves. If the Cohanim are to bless
others with success – then it can only be done with love, the love
of a parent.

And why the Cohanim specifically? Because they are the 2% clan.
The Cohanim were not allowed to own property for themselves,
instead they lived off donations from the rest of the Jewish people.
They received 2% of everything grown by their fellow Jews and that
was their ONLY income. Because of this, their success was directly
linked to the success of the people and so their blessing for others
was genuine and heartfelt.

And what's the meaning of the blessing?

The Rabbis explain this blessing as follows:

i) "May God bless you and keep you" means: "May you be blessed with
MATERIAL wealth and may it not be stolen, lost, or taken from you
(our basic comforts). .

ii) "May God light up your face and be gracious to you" means: "May
you be enlightened by the light of Torah knowledge and understanding" – the blessing for UNDERSTANDING (our psychological needs).

iii) "May God lift up His face towards you and may He grant you peace"
means: "May you be blessed with Shalom – peace of mind" – the
blessing for SATISFACTION (our self-actualization).

In the early 1940s, a Jew named Abraham Maslow devised a pyramid of human needs. His theory is still used today in the fields of
sociology, psychology and management.

He proposed that there are different levels of human needs in life,
ranging from the most basic (physical needs) to the more sophisticated (self esteem through acquisition of knowledge). At the highest
level of human needs, Maslow placed self- actualization, or fulfillment.

---

1.   This is based on a discussion by my teacher, Rabbi Shlomo Riskin.

There is a clear parallel between Maslow's theory and the Priestly Blessing that dates 3,500 years prior to his book. But there is one fascinating difference.

Maslow draws his pyramid with the basic human needs of material goods at the bottom and the highest level – self-fulfillment – at the top.

The Midrash comments on the geometric format of the blessing. There are three words in the first blessing for material goods, five in the second for understanding, and seven words in the third blessing for self-fulfillment.

What transpires is that the blessing forms a sort of pyramid, but with self-fulfillment at the bottom and material needs at the top. Exactly the inverse of Maslow's pyramid!

While Maslow was describing human needs from a perspective of physical priorities (i.e., there is no value in understanding or fulfillment if you can't afford to put bread on the table), the Priestly Blessing is describing these needs in order of spiritual importance.

May God bless you and keep you

יְבָרֶכְךָ ה' וְיִשְׁמְרֶךָ:

May He light up His face to you and be gracious to you

יָאֵר ה' פָּנָיו אֵלֶיךָ וִיחֻנֶּךָּ:

May God lift up His face towards you and give you peace

יִשָּׂא ה' פָּנָיו אֵלֶיךָ וְיָשֵׂם לְךָ שָׁלוֹם:

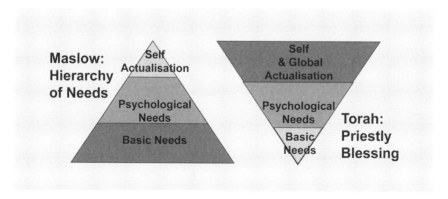

Fig 2.4 Maslow and the Priestly Blessing

And in terms of putting God in the center of our circles, the Priestly Blessing ends with the word Shalom – the greatest achievement one can obtain in life is inner peace and playing one's own part in progressing world peace.

Chapter 56

TRUMAH –
DON'T FORGET THE FOOD

There are a number of rituals that are related to donating food to the Temple. These include:

i) *Trumah* (donation) – 1% of produce that would be separated by a farmer and given to the Cohanim

ii) *Maaser* (tenth) – 10% of produce separated annually by a farmer for the Levites

iii) *Trumat Maaser* (donation from the tenth) – 10% of the *Maaser* portion separated by the Levites for the Cohanim (i.e., another 1% of the initial produce)

iv) *Challah* – a small part of one's dough taken off while making bread and given to the Cohanim (in Temple times), today wrapped and disposed of

v) *Maaser Sheni* (second tenth) – a second 10% of one's produce separated for one's own consumption – in Jerusalem – taken in years 1,2,4,5 of the seven-year Sabbatical cycle.

vi) *Maaser Ani* (poor tenth) – given in years 3 and 6 of the seven-year Sabbatical cycle – 10% of one's produce to the poor.

Accordingly, in Temple times, the tax rate was 11%–21% consisting of:

1% (directly) to the Cohanim,

10% to the Levites and

10% to the poor (every three years of the cycle – or for one's own consumption in Jerusalem in the other years).

What was the meaning of these gifts?

There's a Jewish tale:

> An old man, on his deathbed, summons his four sons to his side and says, "To Reuven and Shimon, my financially astute sons, I leave all my money. To Levi and Yehuda, my less competent sons – I leave nothing!" All four sons are shocked about the unfairness of the situation. Then the father says, "I leave my money to Reuven and Shimon, because I also leave them with the responsibility for looking after their brothers."

The message of this tale is that God grants wealth to those whom He expects to look after others, including the poor, the priestly caste, or even members of one's own family.

The message of these gifts is simply: our possessions are not our own.

Our possessions are a temporary gift from God for us to use for the best purpose we can. For a Jew, money and wealth must be an EN-ABLER but never a symbol of status. Wealth confers responsibility, not just self-gratification.

A people charged with changing the world cannot be hankered by lack of funds – so funds must be pooled for the greater good.

Overall, the **Ritual** category is full of commandments that require us to perform acts that speak to our soul and accustom us to become the people that we are required to be in order to transform the world.

Chapter 57

ACTS OF KINDNESS – GOING OVER AND ABOVE

The three classes of mitzvot which are solely commanded to Jews are **Prayer**, **Rituals**, and **Acts of Kindness**.

Commandments in the class of **Prayer** consist of activities that prepare the mind for making peace. **Rituals** consist of activities that infuse our souls with the deepest meaning of peace.

The final class of commandments which the Torah only proscribes for Jews, is termed **Acts of Kindness**. These are commandments that require Jews to act with a higher level of care (for one another) than required by the world as a whole.

These **Acts of Kindness** create a Jewish community that is an example to all around. A people who are tasked with changing the world for the better must live a life that is demonstrably more enriched than elsewhere and must show a level of care and respect for one another that is a level above those whom they must inspire.

Commandments in this category include:

i) Charity

ii) Visiting the sick and elderly

iii) Teaching the uneducated

iv) Getting married, raising children, and educating them in a stable home

Importantly, most of these commandments have been adopted, over the past 2,000 years, by other cultures, and so today they are not seen as exclusively Jewish values. That demonstrates the success of "leading by example."

Chapter 58

MARRIAGE – A GREAT JEWISH GIFT TO THE WORLD

Marriage is not usually considered a Jewish law. Most people would see it as perfectly normal in modern society that a man and woman would get together and commit to each other for the benefit of creating a stable home environment for their own benefit and for the benefit of their offspring.

However, this was not always the case. Our Rabbis taught:

> "Before the Torah was given, a man would meet a woman at the marketplace and, if she consented, take her into his home. Once the Torah was given, a marriage had to be perfomed before witnesses . . ." (Rambam, "Laws of Marriage," Chapter 1)

Prior to the Torah, couples would get together without much prior commitment (and part with the same lack of effort). The modern institution of marriage with its formal and public ceremony, owes its origins to the Torah. In our "modern" world where one-night-stands have become commonplace, we have not necessarily progressed dramatically from this situation of three millennia in the past. In the words of one great Rabbi[1] "the new morality. . . . is just the old immorality!"

But what is the benefit of a committed couple relationship (i.e., marriage)?

Says the Rambam:

> "It is well known that people require [the love of] friends during their lifetime. . . . This love is more frequent and intense between parents

---

1.   The late Rabbi Alan Unterman of Richmond Synagogue

and children, and among [other] relations. Perfect love, brotherhood, and mutual assistance is only found among those near to each other by relationship . . . prostitutes were therefore not tolerated in Israel (Deut. xxiii. 18), because their existence would disturb the relationship between people. Their children are strangers to everybody; no one knows to what family they belong; nor does any person recognize them as relatives. And this is the greatest misfortune that can befall any child or father . . ." [2]

In other words, society requires stable families where children know their fathers and fathers take responsibility for their children. The love that emanates from family relationships surpasses all other forms of love. That is the love that creates happiness and enables us to perform good deeds.

But there is another major benefit of marriage, specifically of the marriage contract.

The first couple relationship in the Torah is between Adam and Eve. When Eve is first introduced to Adam, she is introduced by God with a strange term: she is an *"ezer ke'negdo"* – literally "a helper against him."[3]

The Rabbis ask, "What does this apparently contradictory term mean? Surely she is either a helper or she is against him, how could she be both?!!"

And they answer,

> *"If he deserves her, she helps him. If not, she argues with him."*
> Alternatively, *"If he deserves her, she argues with him, if not she hits him!"* (*Babylonian Talmud Yevamot* 63a).

The first answer is logical – the Torah is describing a relationship where the wife's behavior is a direct reaction to the way that she is treated by her husband. And the message is clear: "it is the husband's responsibility to treat his wife with love and respect in order for her to respond in kind."

However, at first glance, the second answer is surprising. If he merits, she argues with him! According to this opinion, the best outcome of

---

2. *Guide to the Perplexed*, Rambam, Chapter 49
3. *Bereishit*, 2:18

a marriage is that you have a wife who constantly challenges you! This turns out to be a very deep insight into marriage.

A single man has no one who will tell him the truth about himself. His parents will tell him how wonderful he is (even when he's not). His siblings will take a certain level of interest in him, but they have their own lives and eventually may move out of town. His friends are his friends only as long as they get on well, but a friend who is overly critical of his lifestyle or life choices will very soon be an ex-friend. So who can tell him the truth about himself? The answer: only his wife! And, similarly, the only person to tell a woman the truth about herself is her husband.

While they are dating, the couple will generally be very complimentary to one another; overcome by romantic love, they can see only the good. But very soon after marriage, the couple realizes that they have made a life-long commitment. If she can't stand the way he leaves his toothpaste around the sink, she'll eventually tell him. If he can't stand the way she leaves the house a mess, he'll eventually have to tell her. If she thinks he's wasting his life in a dead-end job and not pushing himself out of his comfort zone, she'll end up telling him. And if he wants her to be more hospitable to his parents, eventually he'll have to say something too.

A healthy husband-wife relationship is one of the few relationships a person has that can be entirely honest. When you know you're living with someone for the rest of your life, you may as well come out and say what you're really feeling! And that has positive repercussions for both husband and wife, helping them to truly fulfill their potential in life. It's like having a life coach living with you.

But, physiologically, this relationship is not equal. A man can impregnate a woman and continue to earn a living. A woman who is pregnant or feeding cannot continue to work, at least for a few months. And if she doesn't have a solution to child care, it could be difficult for her to re-enter the workplace even after a few years. So in primitive societies, where wives were given no rights, the ability of the woman to state her own views, about the husband, was truly limited.

Hence, perhaps the greatest innovation of the Torah, in the field of family law, was the marriage contract – a contract that guarantees the wife an income in the case of the death of her husband or in the case of divorce. The marriage contract, that some see as an unfair burden on a husband, actually evens the playing field between man and wife. With the guarantee of support, at least for the number of years that she cannot return to work, the marriage contract evens out the natural, physiological imbalance of power in the marital relationship. It is, therefore, the marriage contract that enables the husband and wife to exert an equal power within the relationship to change each other for the better.

Marriage is an essential institution to create stable family and community. The marriage contract itself is a vehicle for equality that can lead to a greater degree of self-fulfillment for both husband and wife.

Marriage is an example of a commandment in the category **Acts of Kindness**, which sets an example to the world of the benefit of morals and goodness.

Chapter 59

TZEDDAKAH – LEARNING HOW TO GIVE

Another **Act of Kindness** commanded to Jews is charity, or in Hebrew "*tzeddakah.*"

A Jew is required to give between 10%–20% of his or her income to charity.

We learn this from our forefather, Jacob. When Jacob had his dream about a ladder stretching to heaven, he made a commitment to God,

> *"Out of everything You give me, I will surely tithe it (aseir asireinu)"*
>
> *(Bereishit 28:22)*

And the Talmud, picking up on the double language "aseir asireinu" comments,

> *"One who gives charity should not give more than 20%, as it says "aseir asireinu" – 10% and another 10%."* *(Babylonian Talmud Ketuvot 50a)*

Rashi explains,

> *"In order that he does not become a charity case himself."*

From this we learn that the ideal of charity is to help others while not endangering one's own livelihood.

And the challenge of charity, is precisely that. It is difficult to give money without begrudging the loss of income to oneself. Consider taxes. We might agree with supporting others in theory, but we resent paying taxes in practice.

This is especially true with taxes paid from money we have in our pocket.

We resent council taxes that we pay by check, because we have to part with money that was already in our possession. Somehow the pain of income tax, deducted at source, is less, because the money never actually hit our wallet – we never really counted it as our own.

So with Jewish charity – *tzeddakah* – the ideal is to separate the money from ourselves in the least painful way, in order to distribute it, with joy, to others in need.

When the Jewish people were asked to make their first donation to the *Mishkan* (the portable Temple they carried around the desert), the Torah writes,

> *"Speak to the children of Israel, and have them take for Me a donation"*   (Shemot 25:2)

And the Rabbis ask the simple question, "Why does the Torah ask us to **take** a donation and not, simply, to **give** a donation?"

And the answer is illuminating. The process of giving charity involves two major stages.

i) *Taking* the money out of our pocket and, then

ii) *Giving* it to the poor and needy

The most difficult stage is the first. Taking our hard-earned money from ourselves, separating it from the rest of our spendable resources, is psychologically challenging. And that's why the Torah stresses this part of the action.

In practice, today, one can automatically sweep 10% of one's income from one's pay check into a separate "charity" account. Once it is in that account, one can derive tremendous pleasure in allocating the money to worthy causes.

The Hebrew word for charity, "*tzeddakah*," literally means "justice." Whereas the word "charity," derived from the Latin word "caritas" refers to "generosity" and implies a voluntary act of kindness, the Hebrew word implies the fulfillment of an obligation, the redistribution of God's funds that were never ours in the first place.

Interestingly, the quantitative requirement of *tzeddakah* is between

10%–20% as explained above. This relates to a fraction of approximately 1/7th (15%).

The fraction of 1/7th should already be familiar to us from a number of other places within the Torah:

i) Shabbat comprises 1/7th of the week

ii) The Sabbatical year is 1/7th of all years

iii) Festivals and fast days take up 1/7th of the Jewish year[1]

In other words, for a Jew, 6/7th of one's time and resources are for oneself. But 1/7th is for God. And God commands us to spend 1/7th of our time dedicated to remembering His role in creation and to give 1/7th of our financial resources to support His other creations.

---

1. Pesach, Shavuot, and Succot comprise 16 days in the Torah. Add 9 days for Chanukah and Purim, 17 days for Rosh Chodesh (excluding Rosh Hashana but including two days Rosh Chodesh six times a year), 10 days of Repentance (these include Rosh Hashana and Yom Kippur) – this amounts to 52 days out of a Jewish year that comprises a nominal 355 days (note the Gematria of שנה is 355).

Chapter 60

VISITING THE SICK – AND KNOWING WHAT TO SAY

Another commandment in the category of **Acts of Kindness** is that of visiting the sick and elderly.

It is not sufficient to just give money to support institutions for the sick and elderly (although this, in itself, is a good fulfillment of the commandment for charity). One needs to visit the sick as well.

The Rabbis write,

> *"Visiting the sick removes a portion of their illness"*
>
> (Babylonian Talmud, Nedarim 29b)

Rashi explains that this is 1/60th of the illness.

Whatever the statistical benefit is to the ill person, it is clear that they benefit from the social contact, at a time when many people may be inclined to stay away.

But there is a very practical side to visiting the sick.

> *"When visiting a sick person it is important to examine the room in which he/she is laying to ensure that it is clean, neat and not dusty and that he/she isn't lacking any food, medicine or supplies to aide in their recovery. Doing these things are not just supplemental to the Mitzvah of visiting, rather this is the primary fulfillment of the Mitzvah, as a cluttered room can cause a sick person's state to worsen and by tidying up can cause his situation to improve.*
>
> (Based on the actions of Rabbi Akiva related by the Babylonian Talmud Nedarim 40a)

In fact, it is a mitzvah to ask the sick person if one can assist in any of their needs.

There is a story that occurred during the last intifada in 2000.

> *A remote Peruvian community of South American Indians, who became fascinated with Judaism and Israel, began the long process of conversion in the late 1990s.*
>
> *Four of their members managed to convert and move to Israel, but the vast majority were unable to afford the long process of conversion that had to take place in the distant capital city, Lima.*
>
> *In 2000, one of the converts who had moved to Israel was sitting on a bus in Jerusalem that was blown up by a suicide bomber. Taken to Hadassah hospital in a critical condition, he was visited by the then Chief Rabbi, Meir Lau. Rabbi Lau asked him if there was anything he could do for him (probably expecting him to ask for more comfortable pillows or better food) and he was given the astonishing answer, "Yes! Please would you help the rest of my Peruvian village to convert and come to Israel!"*
>
> *Soon after this hospital visit, Rabbi Lau led a consortium of rabbis to Peru where they spent two weeks in the small village, converting ninety men, women, and children. The community now lives in Alon Shevut, South of Jerusalem.[1]*

Caring for the poor, sick, and elderly is a defining feature of Judaism and every civilized culture in today's world. But astonishingly, it was frowned upon by Roman civilization and even more recently by philosophers such as Nietzsche.

Nietzsche criticised Judaism as a "slave morality."[2]

> *"The Jews achieved a miracle in the inversion of values . . .they made 'poor' a synonym for 'holy' . . . the slave revolt in morals begins with them."*   (Nietzsche, On the Genealogy of Morals)

For Nietzsche, it was the Jewish people who made it acceptable to be poor or sick, and hence challenged the status of "might" over "right." It was Jews who inverted the Darwinian concept of survival of the fittest.

Nietzsche lauded, instead, the "morality" of the master race,

---

1. Story heard from Rabbi Shlomo Riskin in 2004 and printed in part in the Guardian newspaper, 7th Aug, 2002.
2. Friedrich Nietzsche, Trans. by Helen Zimmern (1909-1913).

> *"Life is, to my mind, about growth, survival and the accumulation of force and power: where the will to power is lacking there is decline. . . ."*[3]

It is not surprising that Adolf Hitler was a keen follower of Nietzsche's philosophy.

Today, most civilized people in developed nations would consider that caring for others in need is a key moral objective. Indeed, over the past century, the establishment of socialized healthcare, schooling, and welfare payments has become the norm in all Westernised countries.

Charity and caring for others are two important commandments in the category **Acts of Kindness** that set an example to the world in how to take responsibility for all of mankind.

---

3.   *The Portable Nietzsche*, ed. & trans. W. Kaufmann, New York: Viking, 1954.

Chapter 61

ISRAEL – THE GLOBAL CENTER FOR PEACE STUDIES

One of the 613 commandments is to live in the land of Israel.[1]

The Rambam writes:

> It is forbidden to leave the Land of Israel except in order to learn Torah, or to marry, or to escape from persecution – after which one must return to the Land. One may also leave for business. To live outside Israel is forbidden, unless there is a severe famine . . . and, even then, it is not righteous conduct.[2]

Other statements from our Rabbis confirm the importance of living in the land of Israel.

> "Living in the Land of Israel is the equivalent of all the Mitzvot in the Torah"
>
> (Sifrei, Parshat Re'eh)

> "One should rather live in the Land of Israel in a city where the majority are idol worshippers, than in the Diaspora in a city where the majority are Jews."
>
> (Babylonian Talmud Ketubot 110b)

> Why did Moses yearn to enter the Land of Israel? Did he need to eat its fruits, or to indulge in its bounty? Rather, Moses said: "The people of Israel have been given many commandments, and they cannot be fulfilled except in the Land of Israel."
>
> (Babylonian Talmud Sotah 14a)

---

1. According to the Ramban
2. Rambam, "Laws of Kings" 5:9

But why should living in Israel be such an important mitzvah? Rav Abraham Isaac Kook believed that the Jewish return to the Land of Israel was a critical stage in God's plan for world redemption.

> *It was clear to Rav Kook: such redemption could only be carried out within the framework of a Jewish state. The Jewish people needed a state of their own. Only in a state could they return to the divine and national way of life that God had commanded them. The true glory of God's name could not be expressed when it was confined to the study houses and synagogues of the Diaspora and limited to the world of the spirit. It needed to expand to the full dimensions of national life.*

> *Moreover, Judaism itself needed to reflect every area of that national life. To Rav Kook, Judaism was not limited to prayer and study. It was a full three-dimensional way of life that penetrates the physical and the spiritual together, as one. . . . It was a perversion of Judaism to limit oneself to the world of study. Judaism is unlimited in the world of life. This only happens within a Jewish state . . .[3]*

In other words, all the commandments discussed in this book are best performed within a Jewish state. A Jewish state is the best environment for Jews to incubate peace.

So what is it about the Land of Israel that makes it so critical for Jews, from all over the world, to live there? What's wrong with New York, Paris, or London? And how do Jews living in Israel better transform the world and bring it to a state of Messianic redemption – i.e., peace?

The answer is that Israel finds itself in the middle of Global tension, today and in history.

On its western border, Israel connects to Egypt and North Africa, the location of wars throughout the 20th century. On its eastern front, Israel is separated from the warring nations of Iran and Iraq by Jordan, its (now) peaceful neighbor. In the north, Israel is bordered by Lebanon and Syria – two centers of global terrorism, sponsored by Russia and Iran, and in the south, Israel is close to Saudi Arabia, a close ally of America, armed to the hilt to combat its Soviet-backed neighbors.

The political situation in the Middle East can be described as an

---

3.   From www.hertzl.org.

internecine war between Arab nations, augmented by an international tension due to the involvement of Russia, the United States
and NATO nations.

And Israel is right in the middle of this.

And always has been. Consider how many empires have conquered
Israel over the past three and half millennia.

Period	Empire
1,500 BCE	Jewish (Joshua through to First Temple)
586 BCE–538 BCE	Babylonian
538 BCE–516 BCE	Persia
516 BCE–174 BCE	Jewish (Second Temple)
174 BCE–135 BCE	Greek (and then Hasmonean, Jewish)
135 BCE–60 CE	Jewish
60 CE–390 CE	Roman
390 CE–611 CE	Byzantine
611 CE–636 CE	Persian
636 CE–1099 CE	Arab
1099 CE–1260	Crusader
1260 CE–1517 CE	Mamluk
1517 CE–1920 CE	Ottoman
1920 CE–1948 CE	British
1948 CE–	Jewish

*Table 3 – Domination of Israel under different
empires 1,500 BCE to the present*

But how can Israel be a center for Peace when it is surrounded by
warring nations?

And that's precisely the point.

Peace-making is an abstract thought when you live in a serene region. Making peace on the streets of Rome or Wisconsin is not a
full-time occupation. But making peace in the Middle East is the
beginning of spreading peace across the entire world. And who is
best suited to this peace-making activity?

Israel. At the heart of the war zone. With its Jewish citizens who
have been entrusted with spreading an ideology of world peace
across the globe.

And the in-gathering of the exiles, so anticipated by Jews for the past two millennia, strangely provides the solution to ending world conflicts. This is represented in our daily *Amidah* prayer by the positioning of our pleas to God:

i) The first communal request: Bring back the Jewish exiles from around the world to Israel

ii) The final prayer: Bring peace to the world

Our (communal) pleas begin with a request for the ingathering of Jewish exiles back to Israel and end with a request for Global Peace.

But, how will the return of Jews to Israel lead to Global Peace?

Well, the mix of nationalities in Israel is greater than any other nation. This is due to the relatively recent repopulation of the country through immigration over the past seventy years.

Jews have returned (and continue to return) to Israel from Europe, America, Africa, and the Middle East, not to mention South America, Australia and the rest of the world.

This has created many tensions over the years. Perhaps the greatest tension was between Ashkenazim and Sefardim, Jews from European (i.e. Christian) countries and Jews from Arab (i.e. Muslim) countries. These tensions are still being ironed out in Israeli society, but strangely make Israel the most experienced nation in the art of integrating Eastern and Western cultures.

Add to this that around 20% of Israeli citizens are Muslim Arabs, many of whom do not support the concept of a Jewish State, then peace-making within the borders of Israel becomes a microcosm of peace-making around the Middle East and the Globe.

The system of government in Israel, with multiple interest-based political parties, allows each group to participate at a National level, creating a political structure that accommodates the needs of the majority.

Logically, if God were to choose a nation to be in charge of spreading Global Peace, He would place it right in the middle of all the conflict zones – in the Land of Israel.

And Israel has contributed and continues to contribute to Global Peace in a unique way:

i) The democratic system of government in Israel is a role model for all Middle Eastern nations.

ii) Israel has been nominated, by polls of its 1.5 million plus Arab citizens, as the freest country in the Middle East for an Arab to live.[4]

iii) It has been argued that the nascent trend towards democracy (the Arab Spring) is precisely due to the experience of Arab Israelis spreading across the region.

iv) The Israeli army and intelligence organizations are at the front of the war on global terror, working hand in hand with NATO forces to eliminate terror in the region and around the world.

v) Israel, through being so local to terrorist states, is frequently the first target of Global Terror. Its techniques in combating terror, therefore, are frequently used as a template for other nations to follow.

---

4. According to the Israeli Democracy Index, a public opinion project conducted by the Guttman Center for Surveys and the Israel Democratic Institute. Albeit that Israeli Arabs also believe that they are treated as second-class citizens.

Chapter 62

SUMMARY

"Those who create animosity have hatred in their hearts, whilst those who drive peace have happiness." (Proverbs 12:20)

We asked two questions, "How does the Torah transform my life for the better?" and "How does the Torah transform the world for the better?"

We answered the first question by showing how the Torah commandments lead to a life of happiness – since it commands all the components that drive happiness such as a focus on family, community, time off, and a meaningful occupation.

We answered the second question, "How does the Torah transform the world for the better?" by showing how everything that a Jew is commanded is ultimately to bring the world to a state of peace, Shalom.

So we could rightfully ask two further questions, "If the Torah commands happiness, how can it also command peace? And if the Torah commands peace, how can it also command happiness?"

The answer is clear. In the words of the Maharal (16th Century Prague),

> *Peace (Shalom) is about creating completeness (sheleimut). And when we feel complete, then we are happy.*[1]

In other words, peace and happiness are two sides of the same coin. When I am at peace, I am happy and when I am happy, I will act to create peace.

---

1. Maharal of Prague, *Netivot Olam*, Shalom.

The Jewish people have been given an incredible set of commandments that both create peace and happiness. The Torah is our heritage, our responsibility and our delight.

Section 3

THE FUTURE

Chapter 63

THE DESTINATION–
MESSIANIC TIMES

How do Jewish sources see the world progressing into the future?

The Prophets and the Rabbis of the Talmud foretold of a Messianic era that would lead to Global Peace.

"The world will stand for six thousand years – two thousand years of nothingness, two thousand years of Torah and two thousand years of the Messianic Era – due to our sins, most of this period has expired."[1]

Since the Jewish counting of years begins from Adam and Eve, the year 6000 relates to the Secular year of 2239 – or just over 200 years from now.

According to our principle sources, the Messianic era must occur by then. Given that some babies born today will live over 115 years, and assuming that the human lifespan will not contract over this period, it is likely that someone who is alive in the Jewish year 6000 will be a great-great-grandchild of someone born today and will have sat on their lap! That's how close our generation is to the final redemption!

And the source for this?

The Ramban explains[2] that the sequence of events during the six days of Creation is a template for the unfolding of history over six millennia:

> On the first two days of Creation light and water were created. These
> represent the first thousand years of Creation where man was created

---

1. Babylonian Talmud *Avodah Zarah* 9b.
2. Commentary on *Bereishit* 2:3.

(who lit up the world with knowledge of God) and the water of the flood that occurred in the second millennium.

On the third and fourth days of Creation, the plants, sun and moon were created. The plants represent the flowering of world religion after Abraham came to recognize God, during the third millennium, and the sun and moon represent the First and Second Temples that were built (and destroyed) in the fourth millennium.

On the fifth day of Creation, the fish and birds were created and multiplied hugely. These represent the growth of nations and cultures in the world during that period (300 CE – 1,300 CE).

On the sixth day of creation, animals and man were formed. The animals represent the violent wars that would take place throughout the millennium. But man, who was created just before dusk on the sixth day, represents the Messianic era where all of mankind will once more "know" God.

But how will we know that the Messianic period has arrived?

Says Rabbi Shmuel, in the Babylonian Talmud *Brachot* 34b,

> *"There will be no difference between the Messianic era and today except that Jews will rule over Israel."*

And Rashi adds:

> *"When the Land of Israel bears its fruits in abundance . . . there is no greater sign."*

These sources teach us that the Messianic era will have arrived when Israel is once again ruled by Jews and when the land starts to bear fruit after millennia of being dried up.

Thank God, we live in this period.

The Babylonian Talmud[3] tells us further:

> *In the build-up to the Messianic era, chutzpah will grow, inflation will be oppressive, there will be plenty of grapes but wine will be expensive (Rashi: because everyone will be throwing parties),*

---

3. Sotah 49b.

governments will turn to heresy, and no one will rebuke them (because people will say "who are YOU to rebuke ME?!"). Schools will be used for debauchery, the Galilee will be burned, the Golan will lie desolate and citizens from the [Northern] borders will shift from town to town and not stop wandering. The wisdom of the Sages will offend, those who fear sin will be loathed. Truth will be abandoned, the young will embarrass the old, and the old will stand before the youth. A son will disgrace his father and a daughter rise up against her mother, a daughter-in-law before her mother-in-law. One's family will become one's enemy. The face of the generation will be like the face of a dog (i.e., the leaders will look to the people for direction); a son will not be embarrassed before his father. So, on whom will we be able to rely? Only on our Father in Heaven.

Say our Rabbis: things will get worse before they get better.

According to this source, the signs of the Messianic era will be:

A modern culture that loses respect for conventional wisdom.

A society where the family structure breaks down and one's home becomes a place of anxiety rather than rest.

A time when leaders look back to the electorate for the direction in which to lead.

Sounds familiar?

Says the Talmud, only when things get so bad, will the Messianic period begin.

Why do things have to get worse before they get better?

The Midrash teaches:

> *The Torah is acquired in three places – in fire, in water, and in the desert.*

In other words, we Jews reattach to our culture in three ways.

i) Through fire – sometimes grabbed by an eloquent and charismatic speaker or writer, one can change one's life in an instant – like a fire that sweeps over us. But like a fire the passion can die down very fast.

ii) Through water – like the water that changed the life of Rabbi Akiva.

The Midrash tells us about the uneducated forty-year-old shepherd Akiva who sat one day by a waterfall. Keen to learn, but fearing that he was too old to start, Akiva watched as a side stream dripped constantly onto a hard rock. Noticing that the rock had a marked indentation where the dripping had eroded it over many years, Akiva said to himself, "If water, which is soft, can chisel through hard rock, then the Torah, the water of life, can chisel through my hard heart!" He then started a twenty-four-year program of learning that led him to become the greatest Rabbi of his generation. We, too, can acquire Torah through "water" – the long, painstaking process of learning and imbibing from our teachers. And the result is long lasting.

iii) Through the Desert – if acquiring Torah through fire is fast but not necessarily long lasting, and acquiring Torah through water is slow but sustainable what, then, is the acquisition of Torah "through the desert"?

We live in a generation where the moral culture around us is like a desert. We live in a vacuum of values, an emptiness of ethics, and a paucity of principles. The messages that the media present to us are mostly salacious, titillating, and generated to make us feel incomplete unless we buy the latest iPhone, 3D TV, or console. In this environment, the Torah stands like a luscious oasis in the midst of a dry wilderness. The Torah can be discovered because it's just the thing we were looking for, but we never knew it existed.

The Messianic era will arrive just when we see society descend to its lowest ebb, because that's when we will want it the most.

And when people, i.e., you and me, want to see peace in the world, that's when we will get together and make it happen.

Chapter 64

OUR GENERATION –
MESSIANIC FOOTSTEPS

Life today is moving at a faster pace than ever.

We are in constant touch with business colleagues, customers, friends, and family through our smart phones. Not only do we have up-to-the-minute knowledge of events that are occurring around the world through news channels, but we can even get first-hand, personal reports of major incidents videoed by someone on the scene and tweeted round the world in an instant. And we can work and communicate with people we've never met, who live the other side of the globe.

And this greater knowledge of the world has all the potential to lead us to a greater understanding of others, to greater levels of tolerance, and therefore to a greater understanding of God.

And sometimes it does. We see evidence of this when world disasters bring in increasingly more money from individual donors[1] who feel like they are witnessing the disaster first-hand, minute-by-minute, as it unfolds. We see evidence of this when nations send increasingly large peace-making forces to warzones. We see evidence of this when charities and governments increasingly work cross-border to solve disease and poverty.

The development and dissemination of the phonetic alphabet was the greatest leap forward in human knowledge and human communication of all time, and this occurred just before the writing of the greatest book of all time, the Torah.

---

1. *Private funding: An emerging trend in humanitarian donorship*, Velina Stoianova, April 2012.

Literacy has been the greatest tool for bringing people to Monotheism, to the tolerance and appreciation of others. Literacy has enabled the teaching of Biblical concepts, and education has enabled people to connect with a bigger picture of reality.

The combination of literacy and Torah has enabled Jews to spread an understanding of Monotheism across the globe, even to places where it is not currently practiced.

Three and a half thousand years later, the next major leap in human knowledge and communication is occurring by means of the internet. The internet has the potential to close the loop and bring an appreciation of Monotheism to all. Two good examples of this are Google and Facebook.

Google has provided the world with a way to have all possible information at our fingertips. And this centralization and greater accessibility of knowledge has the potential to bring us a greater understanding of others and ultimately of God.

Facebook, on the other hand, has led to a mammoth leap in human connectivity. The ability to connect to "friends" and acquaintances and to friends of friends, across the world, on a moment-to-moment basis can move mountains. Tyrannical regimes have begun to fall due to groups of like-minded people coming together for a common purpose – the Arab Spring is just the beginning of this communication revolution.[2]

Ultimately, the more knowledge we have of life, the more we can appreciate the huge contribution of cultures, other than our own, to the complex pattern of our existence.

Google and Facebook did not have to be founded partly by Jews, but they were.[3] A culture of learning and community implanted in the world's consciousness by the Torah over the past three millennia has led to these companies evolving. The fact that these technologies have been adopted faster than any previous technology in history is testament to the deep needs that they fulfill for knowledge and communication – ultimately the deep needs people have to feel part of a greater whole.

---

2. Facebook and Twitter key to Arab Spring uprisings: report, Carol Huang, June 2011, *The National*, UAE
3. Notably Larry Page, Sergey Brin, and Mark Zuckerberg.

The understanding of the greater whole builds tolerance between peoples and helps us to remove ourselves from the middle of our circles and place God there instead.

Modern technology enables us to create communities, real or virtual, that build connections with others and help to build peace in the world.

We live in exciting times where the possibility for global transformation of society and moral values has been rapidly advanced.

Chapter 65

CONCLUSION – IT'S UP TO US

So, returning to my friend in the Radlett Centre on that cold Yom Kippur afternoon.

"Rabbi, isn't the Torah just an ancient text that is out of date and irrelevant in our modern age?"

I guess my answer is, simply, "No!"

The Torah advocates a way of life that has more relevance today than ever before.

A way of life that brings us happiness, fulfillment, purpose, and peace.

Jews have transformed the world we live in, in ways that we can't imagine. Who, today, could imagine a world without community structures, a weekend, equality for women, compassion for animals, charities, and education?

And peace, that Jewish gift to the world, is no longer just a slogan, it is a way of life for most people in most civilized nations. Yes, there are too many wars on this planet, but gradually, with the help of greater interconnectivity, people are learning the benefits of a peaceful way of life.

As we get further away from the giving of the Torah, those 3,500 years ago, it may be getting more difficult for us to see its light through the fog that we call "reality." But the rewards of a Torah lifestyle are immense and unquantifiable, both to us and to the whole world which it sustains.

Chapter 66

POSTSCRIPT –
THE ULTIMATE BLESSING

The Torah is infinite.

A book about its purpose, and the purpose of its disseminators – the Jewish people, could take numerous perspectives.

This book could have expressed how every mitzvah is simply to deepen our connection with God, or to create a greater understanding of our Creator. It could have stressed the importance of love, fear, respect of God, of others or of ourselves. It could have focused on the Land of Israel or purely on the wisdom of our Sages.

The Rabbis expressed, thousands of years back, that the Torah has seventy faces.

There is an ancient Indian parable about three blind men feeling an elephant. One happens to be feeling the trunk. One is feeling the tail and one is feeling a leg. The first man describes a wide tube that is flexible and hollow. The second argues, "No! It is thin and hairy". The third argues, "No! You're both wrong! It is solid and thick, like a tree trunk." Which man is right? Of course, they're all right! But only the sighted person is able to understand that they are describing three elements of a whole.

This book has attempted to provide just two of the seventy faces of Torah – happiness and peace.

Please God, perhaps with the advent of the internet and the greater access to knowledge and communication, the full seventy faces will gradually become understood, and God's kingdom, a place of peace and tolerance, will be rapidly built on earth. Amen.

AFTERWORD TO THE
NEW EDITION

I am a community Rabbi at heart (or at least the husband of a late, and great, community Rebbetzin), and so I must have the last word.

It has now been some 10 weeks since our family's tragedy, and I have had the opportunity to think some more about the value of Emunah (lit., "trust," or even "loyalty" to God) and Shalom.

Emunah is what has saved our family in this difficult time. In the words of Rabbi Joseph Dov Soloveitchik, Emunah is the ability to ask not "Why?" (לְמָה?) but "For what purpose?" ("לְמָה?"). In the words of my Rebbi, Rav Shlomo Riskin, "Emunah is not believing that what you want to happen will happen, but believing that what happens always happens for a reason (even if you don't understand it)." The Kotzker Rebbi once said, "I would never want to serve a God whose ways were understandable to mere mortals." I concur wholeheartedly.

One of the great gifts that Lucy gave our family was the refusal to have a TV in our home once the kids were born. It never became the central shrine in our living room and we never watched the "news," so we were never brainwashed by its shocking interpretations. Instead, Tefillah, prayer, with its timeless message, became our way to understand how great a world it is in which we live.

This has brought me to the conclusion that the amount of challenge we encounter in life is limited, but the goodness that we experience is infinite. In the words of Rav Efrem Goldberg, "If we wake up in the morning, that means God has a task for us today that even Moshe Rabbeinu (Moses) could not have achieved."

The rising of the sun, the presence of just the right amount of oxygen in the air, the physical properties of water that allow it to be the solvent that keeps us alive, the existence of gravity, our incredible neuro muscular system that allows us to get out of bed, and the list goes on and on. None of this would we have appreciated if we had brought up our children on TV with its messages of death, destruction, and envy.

In fact, following television interviews from my lounge, the cameramen often asked, "Where is your TV?" When they heard that Lucy refused to allow one into the home, they all retorted, "A great decision!" The greatest damage caused by television is not so much the content but the passive belief that it is providing me with all the answers. The TV is not my teacher, thank God. As a Jew, I have great Rabbis to learn from and their books adorn my walls. The answers to all our questions are in those books; however, we would need a million lifetimes in order to read, inculcate, and apply them all.

As far as Shalom is concerned, I would like to change the Oxford English Dictionary's definition of the word as "peace." My understanding has evolved and I would now say that if "Peace" is a mosaic, then "Shalom" is a jigsaw puzzle. What do I mean? Peace requires a high degree of uniformity, just as a mosaic requires every piece to be the same-sized square. Yes, the colors can be different, but the squares are all uniform, 5 mm by 5 mm.

Peace works if there is one predominant culture that can take over the world. The Egyptians tried to impose "Peace," followed by the Greeks, the Romans, the Crusaders, and the Ottomans. They all failed. Mankind is too diverse to accept a concept as feeble as "Peace." But Shalom – Shalom is a jigsaw puzzle. Every piece is completely different in color and shape, and yet the pieces still fit together to make an incredible design that would never have been possible without the complexity of the puzzle.

However, as many of us learned through the years of COVID lockdowns, a 2,000-piece jigsaw puzzle cannot be assembled on a wrinkled tablecloth. It can only be put together once the tablecloth has been ironed flat. The condition for Shalom is the elimination of the "bumps," the elimination of "evil." Yes, there are forces, such as terror, which stand in the way of Shalom. For these forces the solution is not to get them to compromise but to eliminate them in order to allow all the other pieces to fit together. With the "bumps" we will never have Shalom, not ever. Without them, the 2,000-piece puzzle will soon be assembled, to the great relief of all the family. Without the "evil" of terror and terror journalism, the eight billion-piece puzzle of mankind will soon be assembled to the great relief of all the family of (wo)mankind.

I pray three times a day for a world without "enemies." These are the enemies of Shalom. I know it is possible. Evil was put here for a reason, for us to remove it. And due to the "Ikea effect," if we are involved in removing evil and creating Shalom, then we will value it that much more and maintain it forever.

In my original Postscript, I considered that I could have stressed the importance of love, fear or respect of God – rather than Shalom – as the message behind all the commandments. I wrote this because I believed then, that it was forbidden to suggest that, as mere mortals, we could explain God's overall reasoning for the Torah. However, I have since learned the Rambam's statement at the end of his laws of Chanukah: "Great is Shalom, such that the whole Torah was given in order to make Shalom in the world, as it is written, Proverbs (3:17), 'Its ways are ways of pleasantness, and all its paths are Shalom.'" If King Solomon and the Rambam were able to state that the purpose of the Torah was to create Shalom in the world, then who am I to argue?

May the pursuit of Shalom become the focus of all mankind, and may we merit to see the completion of the Divine jigsaw puzzle here on earth.

Amen.

Leo Dee

Sivan 27,5783
June 16, 2023

ABOUT THE AUTHOR

LEO DEE is a former director at a private equity fund who received his rabbinical ordination in Israel. He was a rabbi in a British village in South Hertfordshire where he learned about the importance of Judaism from his community. On April 7, 2023, however, his life changed forever. His beautiful wife Lucy and his two daughters Maia (20) and Rina (15) were brutally murdered by a Palestinian terrorist on the way up to their Passover holiday by the Sea of Galilee. This book is his outlook on life, where he shows how Jewish practice leads to Shalom, in one's soul and in the world. He lives in Efrat with his three remaining children Keren, Tali and Yehuda.

Any feedback about this book?

The author would be delighted to hear from you at his email address: lucy.leo.dee@gmail.com